, Mike

FRIENDLY
FIRE

A
Recovery
Guide

for Believers
Battered by
Religion

FRIENDLY FIRE

A
Recovery
Guide

for Believers
Battered by
Religion

MIKE WARNKE

DEDICATION

To Susan

The struggle has been breathtaking. The pain has been intense. There is a balm in Gilead. He is the Lord, strong to save. You never let me forget that. You helped me rebuild when there were no tools and little material. No wonder everything we do tastes as much like you as it does like me. There are not sufficient words…

"Thank You" 3726 times, and counting. I love you.

Bosco

ACKNOWLEDGMENTS

There were so many walking with me when there seemed to be so few.

To my sweet Jesus. Well, You did it again. You are the glue that binds this all together. Without You, none of the rest of this makes a lick of sense. Yes, You really *do* know. You are so good. Your Word is so true. It works so well in my life.

To my family. Being Honey, Pappy, Poppy, Diddy and Dad is better than anything. I like it better than everything in Wal-Mart. Thank you all for taking the hits and still loving me, no matter what. Thank you for all the laughter in the tears.

To my friends. What can I say? Your soggy shoulders say it all. If you had not been there for me to cry on, I'm not sure what I would have done. There are a number of you and you all know who you are.

To my overseers. Up and down, up and down, up and down. Thank you for never getting off the ride. The road stretches ever onward. Thank you for being there. Thank you for the days ahead.

To every pastor who said, "Sure, Mike, we would love to have you." You opened the doors and let a wounded warrior through. You are the foundation on which Celebrations of Hope rests. It's been hard, fun, and never dull.

To Destiny Image. Thank you for having the guts to sick your necks out for what you believe in. Thank you for believing in me. Libby, Steve, WHEW! Great Job!

To all of you who continued to believe in us, no matter what. You will never know how much that meant. I wish to acknowledge every card, letter and e-mail of support during a very trying time. We are here because you cheered us on.

Grace and Peace

Mike Warnke

ENDORSEMENTS

Oh, how I welcome this fresh word from Mike Warnke. He has certainly earned the right to author this book. I did not know Mike "before" but I have met the man and experienced the ministry "after." *Friendly Fire* is a word of warning, challenge, and hope. Read it and be blessed!

Rich Marshall
Author, *God@Work*

Mike Warnke has offered the Body of Christ a gift of love by writing this book. He has captured the essence of the experience of many sincere followers of Jesus Christ caught in the crossfire between the "ecclesia" and the "koinonia." Chapters Two and Three are worth the entire book. In a genuine and loving spirit, Mike has distilled the basics of the grace of God in Christ in a manner that hits the target of where we seek to live out the gospel we have received. I pray that this new offering from Mike's heart will find a home for healing and encouragement in many hearts across the family of God.

Archbishop Wayne Boosahda
Presiding Bishop, Communion of Evangelical Episcopal Churches

Publisiier's Note

YOU MIGHT BE ASKING YOURSELF, "Why would a publisher run the risk of publishing an author whose past has had so much controversy?" My time with Mike Warnke has resolved any hesitation I might have had. There is no doubt that this man has paid a huge price for the sins he has committed and the mistakes he has made. The words of Paul are true, "… for whatever a man sows, this he will also reap." This is a spiritual principle that cannot be avoided and Mike has reaped the consequences of his actions.

But there are other biblical principles that also apply to our relationships in the Body of Christ. Paul declared, "Brethren, even if a man is caught in any trespass, you who are spiritual, restore such a one in a spirit of gentleness; each one looking to yourself, lest you too be tempted." Unfortunately, the church is very quick to judge a man for his sin rather than to restore a man from his sin. We are quick to draw our gun of criticism and shoot the man who is fallen but too hesitant to fall on our knees in intercession for the man who is hurting.

Fortunately for Mike, there were those who gathered around him and provided the proper spiritual environment that would lead to healing and restoration. It has been a prolonged and arduous journey as Mike has applied himself to the restorative power of the Word of God and opened himself to the scandalous nature of the mercy of God.

This book tells the story of that journey. Its words were written with the understanding that there is still great ground to gain but also with the knowledge that God has come and restored his soul and brought him back from the dead. His story will give great hope and encouragement to the hundreds of thousands who have fallen in the midst of the battle. He will remind them of the grace of God that comes to them in their dark seasons, calling them home, reminding them that Father is standing on the porch awaiting their return.

It is my deepest prayer that this book will reach the hands of hundreds around the world who are desperate to hear the compassionate words of one who has walked in similar paths and has discovered that God was always there, with open arms, waiting for his return.

CONTENTS

FOREWORD

MIKE HAS TAKEN THE TIME to be as transparent about himself, his walk, his setbacks and his comebacks as anyone I have ever known in the ministry. If all were as transparent as he has been, the Body of Christ would experience a depth of healing and unconditional love such as we have never known in recent decades.

One of my most delightful connections in recent years has been with Mike. He still retains that incredible wit and humor that I have always enjoyed; yet he also carries a profound sense of the grace and glory of God. To touch him these days is to touch the heart of a true servant whose intention it is to bring honor to his Master. The apostle John tells us that "grace and truth" were realized in Jesus Christ. In other words, grace and truth go together! The implication is that there is no grace for a lie. Hopefully by now most people know that Mike was falsely accused about his testimony and that indeed Mike carried a true personal history regarding his past onto the comedy stage—where he stood to make us laugh and cry at the same time as he delivered the "k-o" punch of the gospel in his presentations. Those were indeed defining moments, at least for me. Yet, in spite of false accusation, he realized other areas of his life were in need of healing and rebuilding, and the pain of being falsely accused became perhaps the greatest gift of his Christian experience.

You can't be around Mike these days and not be moved to a place of humility and brokeness yourself. He carries himself in such a way that you desire to walk in the same level of child-like sincerity and truth, because God's grace is so evident on he and his wife. I realize that "going big time" is not what the gospel is all about. However, my prayer is that this book—the story of Mike's journey since 1992—will reach a wider audience than he ever reached in his days prior to that defining moment. This was Mike's defining moment, initiated by a refining crisis that set him free from his inner confining limitation and empowered him to walk in the greatness of Christ's total unconditional love, acceptance, and forgiveness. Whatever judgments people may have made about Mike when the accusations began to fly for which they will have to give account, these days when you hear Mike you get the real Mike uncensored and fresh with the touch of grace.

My prayer is that this book will serve as a key to your journey into what matters most!

Dr. Mark J. Chironna
The Master's Touch International Church
Orlando, Florida

Chapter One

ALL MESSED UP WITH NO PLACE TO GO

"I may be a mess, but I'm God's mess."
—*Joyce Meyer*

IT WAS TWO O'CLOCK in the morning. I was standing on the deck in back of my house shivering in the bone-chilling cold. There was no snow, but it was one of those winter nights so cold that the air itself seemed brittle. The sky was crystal clear and the huge disk of the full moon cast an almost day-like brightness on everything.

Lifting my face toward the heavens, I cried out to God, "You know! No matter what anybody else is saying, no matter how it looks, no matter how I feel, You know! Even if nobody else knows, You know! You can see my heart, and You know!"

I was in the middle of the worst period of my life. For nearly 22 years I had reigned as the number-one Christian comedian in the world, performing to sellout crowds around the globe at the rate of 15 to 20 one-night stands every month. Money flowed in like the water over Niagara Falls. My books and tapes were steady best-sellers. I had the means to go any-where or do anything I pleased. I even had my own private plane. Across those years thousands of Christians who attended my concerts got their hearts right with God and thousands more unsaved people came to Christ. I had everything going for me—money, fame, popularity, a successful career, and an effective ministry. It was all anybody could ask for, right?

Then, suddenly, it all fell apart. In the summer of 1992 a Christian magazine published an article that called into question virtually every aspect of my life, my Christian testimony, and my ministry. I was accused of lying about my testimony—in particular about my past involvement with the occult and as a satanist—and of operating a false ministry, seeking to enrich myself under the guise of evangelism.

The fallout was immediate. My concert schedule dried up and disappeared. My record company pulled all my tapes from the stores and cancelled my contract. Many people I thought were my friends were no longer talking to me. For months I was subjected to a very brutal and very public whipping by the media, both Christian and secular. Many voices in the Christian press castigated me for letting down and betraying the Christian community. The secular press seemed only too happy to join in the feeding frenzy. After all, here was another Christian "big shot" humiliated and cut down to size. The onslaught was relentless, and it nearly destroyed me.

At times the stress was so bad that I broke out in hives. I couldn't sleep, my hair came out by the fistful, and I was unable to eat anything that didn't upset my stomach. My whole world came crashing down around me. Within two months, everything I had worked so hard for was gone. From a guy who had his own plane and 50 employees, I was reduced to the point of one day standing in a Kroger grocery store with a coupon for baked beans and a coupon for toilet paper but only enough money for one or the other.

How had all this happened? Were the media reports true? Was I a fake, a charlatan, a deceiver, and a liar? No. I *never* lied about my testimony and I *never* ran a fake ministry. That being said, however, let me hasten to add that all was not right in the Warnke world. God used this whole mess to get my attention. My life was out of control. I had no spiritual accountability. Decisions concerning the ministry were based on the bottom line rather than on spiritual priorities. To put it bluntly, I was out of order. I quickly discovered that, like the foolish man in Matthew 7:26, I had built my "house" upon the sand. When the storm of controversy hit, everything I had built for 22 years suddenly collapsed like a house of cards.

I literally had to walk away from everything and start over. It wasn't easy. In the minds of many I was finished and rightly so. I had disgraced myself, Christian ministry in general, and had brought reproach on the name of Christ. As far as they were concerned I had no further business or place in the ministry.

At first, I agreed with them. How could I possibly go on in the wake of what had happened? The Lord did not let me off the hook that easily, however. With infinite love and tender kindness He showed me that He was not finished with me yet, regardless of what anybody else said.

My road to restoration began by my humbling myself to the biblical process of submitting to the spiritual oversight and accountability of a group of elders. I had to be completely honest with them and agree to abide by their counsel, no matter what. One of the earliest and best pieces of wisdom they gave me was not to fight back. "Don't try to answer your critics," they told me, "or that's all you will ever be doing. Do you want to spend the rest of your life talking about the controversy, or do you want to spend it talking about Jesus?"

I can't begin to tell you how hard it was. Even though I knew I was doing what the Lord wanted me to do to get back to where He wanted me to be, it was still tough. There were times when I felt so alone. The hurt was so deep, the pain so palpable. To most of the Christian community I was *persona non grata*. Even of those few who still supported me, most did not understand my silence. It was early in those dark days when I stood on my deck that cold winter morning and cried to God, "You know!" When I lost everything else, the Lord was still there. He understood what I was going through, and He cared. He sustained me through the worst period of my life. What gave me the confidence to cry out that morning and the courage to continue on was the assurance, the absolute certainty, that Jesus loved me. He was all I had, and He was enough.

"We Have Met the Enemy, and He Is Us"

EARLY ON IN MY ORDEAL I thought that I was the only person who had ever been through anything like that. The more I looked around, however, the more I saw that there were bodies everywhere—mangled, munched, shredded, and crunched people who had been chewed up by the world and the Church, then spat out by the roadside. Through the lens of my own pain I saw, perhaps for the first time, that the Christian landscape is littered with the bodies of bruised and battered believers—the "walking wounded." It's bad enough when Christians are beaten up by the world, but at least Jesus told us to expect that (see Jn. 15:18; 16:33). What's even worse, though, is when we're hit by "friendly fire"—wounds inflicted on us by others in the Body of Christ. Whether or not we deserve those wounds is beside the point. The hurt they cause is especially deep, the pain particularly acute.

In *Pogo*, his popular comic strip of my generation, the late Walt Kelly coined a line that has since entered the general culture: "We have met the enemy and he is us." Clever as that line is, it also describes a sad reality in the Christian community. One of the greatest sins of the Church today is the harm that we so often inflict on one another, both spiritually and emotionally. For some reason we can't seem to get along. The "family of God" is dysfunctional! We fuss and fight, scrap and squabble, more often than not over things that don't really matter for eternity. Sometimes our quarrels turn into full-blown, knockdown, drag-out free-for-alls that leave everyone limping off to lick their wounds.

This is not a new problem. The apostle Paul had to deal with it in Corinth.

> *I appeal to you, brothers, in the name of our Lord Jesus Christ, that all of you agree with one another so that there may be no divisions among you and that you may be perfectly united in mind and thought. My brothers, some from Chloe's household have informed me that there are quarrels among you. What I mean is this: One of you says, "I follow Paul"; another, "I follow Apollos"; another, "I follow Cephas"; still another, "I follow Christ." Is Christ divided? Was Paul crucified for you? Were you baptized into the name of Paul?* (1 Corinthians 1:10-13)

You can hear the bewilderment in Paul's questions. It's as though he's asking, "C'mon guys, what's gotten into you?" Paul devoted his entire first letter to the Corinthians to dealing with their divisions and infighting.

That's a good question for us to think about. What *has* gotten into us? Why do we fight? Why are we so quick to inflict hurt and harm on our brothers and sisters? The reasons are many: legalism, pride, ignorance, stubbornness, tradition, prejudice, a judgmental spirit, a control spirit, selfishness, disobedience, unbelief, an unforgiving spirit, hypocrisy, immorality, and any number of other personal sins. Fights also occur frequently over the question of maintaining doctrinal purity and theological correctness. Sometimes those fights are necessary because solid, Scripture-based doctrine and theology are critically important to the life and health of the Church. If we're not careful, however, our zeal for doctrinal and theological integrity can cross the line into unreasonable and implacable rigidity that leaves many unnecessary human casualties in its wake.

Forgotten in the midst of all this are Jesus' words, "My command is this: Love each other as I have loved you" (Jn. 15:12), and "A new command I give you: Love one another. As I have loved you, so you must love one another. By this all men will know that you are My disciples, if you love one another" (Jn. 13:34-35).

The unbelieving world likes nothing better than to watch Christians beat up on each other; they convince themselves that we have nothing that they either need or want. It's sad but true. We *have* met the enemy and he *is* us. Why are we so worried about the devil? Sometimes we are our own worst enemy.

Welcome to the Real World

A BIG PART OF OUR PROBLEM in the Church stems from our tendency to harbor unrealistic and unreasonable expectations both of ourselves and of others in the Body. When those expectations are not met, disillusionment sets in. Add to that the fact that other believers sometimes land on us hard because we fail to meet *their* expectations, and we're really in a mess.

Disillusionment can be crippling, especially for brand new believers. Does any of this sound familiar? When you first got saved you may have come into the Church very idealistic. You had just had a pristine encounter with Christ. In fact, it may have been the first truly clean experience of your life. There's something about being washed in the blood of Jesus that makes you glisten; it leaves you feeling squeaky-clean. That blood cleansing gave you a whole new vision of everything.

When I was a little boy, I found it difficult to understand why I couldn't see anything clearly. I always had to sit in front of the classroom because otherwise I couldn't see the blackboard. At home I actually had lain under the TV in order to see it. Someone finally had the sense to take me to have my eyes tested. Would you believe it? I needed glasses! That's why everything had looked so fuzzy to me.

How well I remember the day I first got my glasses. I put them on in the doctor's office and then walked outside. Wow! Everything suddenly had sharp outlines, and I saw variations and shades and brilliance of colors that I had never seen before. It was one of the cleanest experiences I have ever had. That clean feeling was simply breathtaking.

That's how you felt when you got saved. Now you come into the Church and you naturally expect everybody else to be that way too. You expect every Christian to be loving, kind, gentle, and understanding. You expect every pastor to be absolutely above reproach. You expect every situation that arises to be dealt with in a Christlike manner. The first time it doesn't happen that way, you're devastated. Disillusionment starts to set in.

One of the first things you learn is that getting saved didn't make you perfect. You still struggle with temptation, evil thoughts, and sinful urges that make you feel guilty. In the wrong kind of setting, some of the people around you may use your guilt to manipulate you. That is a particularly damaging experience, especially when you wise up to the fact that you've been manipulated.

Before long you find out that the people around you are no better than you are. This is a really bad thing because many of us try to live vicariously through the righteousness of others. Being in righteous company makes us feel more righteous, and it's a dark day when we discover that everybody else is just like we are.

You're not in the Church long before a conflict arises. That's when you see other people in the Church griping, complaining, criticizing, stabbing each other in the back and cutting each other's throats. Maybe by this time you even join in on some of it. It hurts to realize that disagreements in the Body of Christ are not always handled in a Christlike manner, because everybody is struggling with their flesh as much as you are.

Then all of a sudden the pastor does something wrong, and you find out that he too is only human. By now you're trying to deal with the reality that things aren't the way you expected them to be. You start to think, *Maybe I was wrong about all of this. Nothing is really any different from before I got saved. I thought I had finally found something that would last, but it didn't. I guess this "church" stuff just isn't for me.* That's when you want to just throw up your hands and hit the road.

There is a lot of that going on in the Body of Christ: disheartened and disillusioned believers who have fallen by the wayside or gone off to other things or jumped back into the

ALL MESSED UP WITH NO PLACE TO GO

river of the world and all its pursuits. I've seen them and I'm sure you have too. You may even be one of them.

It's easy for us to end up bruised and battered in spirit when the reality of life in the Church does not live up to our ideal. Does that mean we should abandon our ideal? Not at all. It simply means that we should temper our idealism with the recognition that everybody is human.

Don't Choke on the Small Stuff

ANOTHER REASON WE IN THE CHURCH are prone so often to beat each other up is because we let little things become big things. Little problems or annoyances in the Church need to be kept in perspective or they can endanger the health and fellowship of the Body. The Song of Solomon says, "Catch for us the foxes, the little foxes that ruin the vineyards, our vineyards that are in bloom" (Song 2:15). Vineyards in bloom represent life and fruitfulness. Little foxes can destroy fruitfulness. In the same way, little problems in the Church that are left unchecked can grow to monstrous proportions and destroy fellowship.

Have you ever seen those warnings that come with children's toys? They say something like, "Caution: This toy is not intended for children under the age of three. Small parts may come off and create a choking hazard." I think we need a similar warning in the Church: "Be careful not to choke on the small stuff."

In many churches small stuff is a big deal. We like to nitpick tiny things and forget more important matters. We focus on the splinter in someone else's eye while ignoring the beam in our own. In the name of religion we are willing to swallow the biggest bunch of malarkey you ever saw in your life, but

25

let somebody across the room do the least little thing wrong and we choke to death on it. We'll let the enemy come in and walk the aisles of our church tearing us apart with lies, innuendoes, suspicion, and gossip, but just let that sister across the way sing out of key (loudly!), and that's all anybody will talk about for the next month. It doesn't matter that she was "making a joyful noise" because of the love of God in her heart.

Some brother walks into church with beer on his breath. Although he has been trying to do the best he can, he still has an accident. But rather than staying home and wallowing in his weakness and failure, he comes to church hoping to find the strength, support, and encouragement he needs to avoid making the same mistake next time. Instead of getting the love and understanding he deserves, he's bombarded by demands to explain why he messed up.

Who comes to church to get bummed out? We can stay at home for that; just turn on the news! If we want to get knocked down and walked on, we can find that on our jobs. We don't come to church to be beaten up but to be lifted up. We come looking to be loved and affirmed. The last thing we need or want is someone else wagging his finger in our face. We get enough of that in the world.

Accountability is one thing; nitpicky faultfinding is another. Properly administered, accountability in the Church is an affirming experience because we are mutually involved with helping each other stay on the straight and narrow and avoid falling into patterns, habits, and lifestyles of sin. Faultfinding, on the other hand, is mean-spirited and destructive and harps on things that don't amount to squat.

A lot of people have started staying away from church because they're tired of explaining themselves to everybody. I've got news for you. We don't owe anybody an explanation for who we are, where we go, what we do, or how we look. I don't owe you an explanation and you don't owe me an explanation. As believers the only thing we owe each other is our love. Paul wrote to the Romans, "Let no debt remain outstanding, except the continuing debt to love one another, for he who loves his fellowman has fulfilled the law" (Rom. 13:8). Peter had this to say: "Above all, love each other deeply, because love covers over a multitude of sins" (1 Pet. 4:8). Loving each other will help us overcome all the trivia. It will help keep us from choking on the small stuff.

I May Be a Mess, but I'm God's Mess

A LOT OF WHAT I HAVE BEEN SAYING comes from my own experience. In many ways it has been a long ten years. Although I've made a lot of progress, there's still a long road ahead of me. Along the way there have been more than a few moments when I just wanted to throw my hands in the air and give up. It wasn't just what others thought of me—I've gotten used to that and have learned to deal with it for the most part. The real nagging question was how to deal with the feelings I had about myself. How could I shake the notion that I was "spoiled goods"?

When all the trouble first started, an overwhelming sense of failure swept over me. I received what was being said of me because it seemed useless to resist. The more I heard, the more I believed until finally I had no sense at all of myself anymore. Surely the Lord was finished with me. I just knew that God wanted no more to do with me than did many of the people who felt I had betrayed them. After all, Jesus had saved me so wonderfully and I had let Him down so horribly! I was lower than snake spit. Worthless to one and all. In short, I was a mess.

Does any of this hit you where you live? Are you bummed out about church because it turned out to be less than you expected? Have you dropped out because you're tired of being criticized for failing to live up to someone else's idea of how you should look or act as a believer?

Maybe you used to have an effective ministry, but now feel that your ministry has failed or even that *you* have failed in your *ministry*. Maybe you made a big mistake and now it seems like no one will let you forget it. They hold it up before you constantly so that you can neither deal with it nor move beyond it. Do you feel like you have screwed up so badly that you can never come back? That you have let God down so completely that you feel ashamed even to pray? Are you so humiliated by your failure that you cannot bear to look at yourself in the mirror or face any of your brothers and sisters in the Body of Christ? Can you count yourself a member of the company of those who are "all messed up with no place to go"?

For a long time that's the way I felt. Then one day I heard a statement from the ministry of Joyce Meyer that changed the whole way I looked at myself. She said, "I may be a mess, but I'm God's mess." That really spoke to me. I realized that no matter how bad things got; no matter how screwed up my life had become; no matter how messed up I was, I still belonged to God. I was a mess, but I was *His* mess. What a joy and a relief it was to know that God had not abandoned me! He had not become disgusted with me and tossed me on the junk heap. The Lord who was able to save me and raise me to life when I was dead in trespasses and sins was able now to lift me up, clean me off, and straighten me out.

Don't let your pain or your hurt or your shame keep you from turning back to God. Children naturally run to their parents when they are hurting or afraid, when they need comfort, or when they simply want a hug or a kiss. We should be the same way with our heavenly Father. His arms are always open for us. No matter what you've done, you still belong to God. At no point does the Lord stop loving you; at no point do you become dispensable or disposable in His eyes. Never does He wad you up and throw you away. As long as you live and breathe, God has a plan and a purpose for you. At no point will He say, when you pray and cry out to Him, "Oh, it's *you* again." No matter what kind of a mess you are, you are still God's mess. No matter how messed up you think you are, God can deal with it. No mess is too big for God to handle.

God Loves Us Because He Loves Us

THERE IS NOTHING WE CAN DO to make God stop loving us, because we never did anything to make Him start. God loves us because He created us. God loves us because He *is* love and it is His very nature to love. God loves us because He loves us! It's that simple. Nothing can ever remove us from His love. As Paul wrote to the Romans:

> For I am convinced that neither death nor life, neither angels nor demons, neither the present nor the future, nor any powers, neither height nor depth, nor anything else in all creation, will be able to separate us from the love of God that is in Christ Jesus our Lord (Romans 8:38-39).

At all times, and especially those times when you feel your life has gone to the dogs, keep your eyes fixed on Jesus. All the stuff you're going through—pain, sorrow, guilt, anger, shame, tears, whatever—is secondary to the fact that Jesus loves you.

Even if every friend you have forsakes you, you still have a friend in Jesus. The key to surviving the pain is to focus not on the pain but on the One who loves you with an undying love.

If there was ever anyone who understood pain, it was David. He also knew how to move beyond his pain by fixing his heart and mind on the Lord.

> *Be merciful to me, O Lord, for I am in distress; my eyes grow weak with sorrow, my soul and my body with grief. My life is consumed by anguish and my years by groaning; my strength fails because of my affliction and my bones grow weak. Because of all my enemies, I am the utter contempt of my neighbors; I am a dread to my friends—those who see me on the street flee from me. I am forgotten by them as though I were dead; I have become like broken pottery....In my alarm I said, "I am cut off from Your sight!" Yet You heard my cry for mercy when I called to You for help. Love the Lord, all His saints! The Lord preserves the faithful, but the proud He pays back in full. Be strong and take heart, all you who hope in the Lord* (Psalm 31:9-12,22-24).

As long as we keep looking at all the bad stuff; as long as we focus on our failures, we will continue to be failures because we will miss the One who can never fail, and who will never fail us. Regardless of what has happened in your life or what anybody else says or thinks, the issue is not between you and them, or even between you, them, and God. It is between you and the Lord—period. The rest of it is just the rest of it.

We need to remember that we are talking about an individual relationship with a very, very personal God. The secret to surviving the bad stuff is to know and take to heart the simple fact that Jesus loves you. He always has and He always will. Nothing you do will ever change that fact.

Even if you're all messed up, you have somewhere to go: to the Lord. He will never turn you away. As long as you are alive and breathing, and as long as Jesus loves you (which is forever!), it is never too late. He can still make you into the person He wants you to be.

George Herbert, a 17th-century English poet and Christian mystic, beautifully expressed the intimate nature and infinite quality of the Lord's love for us:

> Love bade me welcome, yet my soul drew back,
> Guilty of dust and sin.
> But quick-ey'd Love, observing me grow slack
> From my first entrance in,
> Drew nearer to me, sweetly questioning
> If I lack'd anything.
>
> "A guest," I answer'd, "worthy to be here";
> Love said, "You shall be he."
> "I, the unkind, the ungrateful? ah my dear,
> I cannot look on thee."
> Love took my hand and smiling did reply,
> "Who made the eyes but I?"
>
> "Truth, Lord, but I have marr'd them; let my shame
> Go where it doth deserve."
> "And know you not," says Love, "who bore the blame?"
> "My dear, then I will serve."
> "You must sit down," says Love, "and taste my meat."
> So I did sit and eat.

Chapter Two

YES, JESUS LOVES *YOU*

Jesus loves me! this I know,
For the Bible tells me so...
—*Anna B. Warner*

ONE OF THE MOST REVOLUTIONARY concepts in the history of mankind is the idea that there is a God who *loves* us. Equally radical is the notion that this God who loves us also seeks *our* love in return and desires to relate to each one of us individually.

The thought of a personal and loving God is incomprehensible to the sinful, fallen nature of man. Because spiritual blindness prevents the human race from seeing God as He really is, throughout history we have fashioned "god" according to our human perspectives. In essence, we have made "god" in our own image.

The Philistines, the Assyrians, the Babylonians, and other people groups who populated the Middle East during Old Testament times conceived the gods as fierce and bloodthirsty deities who had to be appeased constantly with offerings, frequently involving human sacrifice. The Greeks and the Romans worshiped gods who, though endowed with supernatural powers, were essentially magnified caricatures of humans, possessing the same lusts, passions, and foibles as mere mortals. These deities were capricious, freely using humans as pawns in their continual schemes and plots against one another.

To Buddhists, whatever gods may exist are at best impersonal deities with whom no relationship is conceivable. For the Hindus, the sacred triad of Brahma/Vishnu/Shiva—gods of creation, preservation, and destruction and regeneration—have set human existence into a never-ending cycle of birth, death, and rebirth (reincarnation). Not even Muslims, who worship one god and often refer to him as "Allah the merciful," would ever think of him in intimate and personal terms.

It took a once obscure band of people known as the Hebrews to bring before the world 3500 years ago a new idea: an all-powerful, all-knowing God who was also an all-loving God who sought a personal love relationship with each of His human creatures. A concept as radical as this notion of a personal and loving God was beyond the scope of man's imagination; it could come about only by divine revelation. If we were ever to know the God of love, He would have to reveal Himself to us.

Fortunately for us, God did just that. From the beginning God has been revealing Himself, reaching out in love and grace, and calling people to come to Him. The Bible is the written record of God's activity to restore fallen humanity to relationship with Himself. Genesis 3:8 speaks of God "walking in the garden in the cool of the day," seeking the man and woman whose sin has separated them from Him. Revelation 21:3 records "a loud voice from the throne saying, 'Now the dwelling of God is with men, and He will live with them. They will be His people, and God Himself will be with them and be their God.' " In between lies the full witness of God's work to move mankind from the estrangement of Genesis to the reunion of Revelation. The God of the Bible is a personal God. He is a loving God. The God of the Bible is a relational God who seeks to draw us to Himself.

What the World Needs Now Is Love, *God's* Love

IF THERE IS ANYTHING the world talks about the most, yet understands the least, it is love. By and large, what the world calls love is a far cry from the love revealed in the Bible. For one thing, the world's version of love so often is conditional. As human beings we attach a lot of stipulations to love. We tend to love those who are like us while shunning those who are not. We limit our love to people who are easy to love, and don't even try to love the difficult or the unlovely. Our love for others lasts as long as they live up to our expectations and meet our needs. We love for awhile, but once the luster fades we become bored, and off we go to try to find a new love. The consequences to our society are predictable and tragic. Everywhere we look we see debris: the wreckage of broken loves, broken relationships, broken families, broken homes, and broken spirits.

Much of the so-called "love" in our modern society is self-centered, self-seeking, and focused on lust and the desire for physical pleasure. Just look at the sitcoms on television: Men and women live together yet are not married, and by the end of the season every character on the show has slept with every other character. In our culture love is something you try on for size, then discard when it no longer suits you. Love is something you play at, not something you get serious about. Society's brand of "love" lives for the moment and fears long-term commitment.

35

The Bible reveals love of a very different kind; a love that never fades or goes away; a love that is not here today and gone tomorrow, but lasts forever. Biblical love is eternal because it is inseparably linked with God, who is Himself eternal. Psalm 90:2 says of Him, "from everlasting to everlasting You are God," while First John 4:16 plainly states, "God is love." God is love, and because He is eternal, His love is eternal.

How does God's love compare with that of the world? First of all, the love of God is unconditional. As I said before, we can never do anything to make God stop loving us because we never did anything to make Him start. Some people believe that God turns on His love for us when we receive Jesus and that every time we fail or backslide He turns it off again. That simply is not true. God's love is like a spotlight that never goes out. Although we may at times step in and out of its beam and feel separated from His love because of our own sinful actions and attitudes, the bright light of the love of God is always shining on us. It always has and it always will.

Love is the very nature of God. God's love for us does not depend on who we are or on what we have or have not done, but on who He is. In the Book of Jeremiah the Lord says, "I have loved you with an everlasting love; I have drawn you with loving-kindness" (Jer. 31:3b). Eternal love is unconditional love because it continues regardless of what we do. God does not require us to meet a certain standard of behavior before He will love us, and He doesn't stop loving us just because we screw up.

Secondly, God's love is active and deliberate. God targets us with His love; we are not accidental recipients. In Jeremiah 31:3 God says, "I have *drawn* you with loving-kindness." Jesus told Nicodemus, "For God so loved the world that He *gave* His one and only Son, that whoever believes in Him shall not perish but have eternal life" (Jn. 3:16). From beginning to end, the Bible relates the story of God's deliberate and relentless love pursuit of mankind. It is one of the major themes of Scripture.

In one sense, we could say that the whole Bible is God's love letter to us. The climax of that letter—the greatest proof of all of God's unconditional, active, and deliberate love for us—is Christ's death on the cross. God didn't just say He loved us; He proved it. Jesus said, "Greater love has no one than this, that he lay down his life for his friends" (Jn. 15:13). The very next day He went to Calvary. In his letter to the Romans, Paul stated it this way: "But God shows and clearly proves His [own] love for us by the fact that while we were still sinners, Christ (the Messiah, the Anointed One) died for us" (Rom. 5:8, AMP). Christ died for us *while we were still sinners*. He did not require us to "clean up our act" first. If you ever doubt God's love for you, just look at the cross.

Hilary of Poitiers, a 4th-century church leader, understood the deliberate and unconditional nature of God's love, and expressed it beautifully in this prayer:

> Although I am dust and ashes, Lord, I am tied to you by bonds of love. Therefore I feel I can speak freely to you. Before I came to know you, I was nothing. I did not know the meaning of life, and I had no understanding of myself. I have no doubt that you had a purpose in causing me to be born; yet you had no need of me, and on my own I was of no use to you. But then you decided that I should hear the words of your Son, Jesus Christ. And that as I heard his words, you enabled his love to penetrate my heart. Now I am completely saturated in his love and faith, and there is no remedy. Now, Lord, I cannot change my attitude to my faith; I can only die for it.

God Has Gotten a Bum Rap

GOD HAS GOTTEN A BUM RAP in the world. The devil has blinded and deceived many people into thinking of God as this mean, frowning, horrible being who likes to beat up on us all the time. To them He is a rough taskmaster who sits up in Heaven just waiting for us to make a mistake so He can squash us like bugs or zap us with a lightning bolt. In their minds God's purpose is to throw every possible roadblock in our path to keep us out of Heaven.

The Bible gives us a very different picture. God loves us and has our best interests at heart. Listen to what He says in the Book of Jeremiah:

> *"For I know the plans I have for you," declares the Lord, "plans to prosper you and not to harm you, plans to give you hope and a future. Then you will call upon Me and come and pray to Me, and I will listen to you. You will seek Me and find Me when you seek Me with all your heart"* (Jeremiah 29:11-13).

Does that sound like a God who wants to zap us? God isn't looking for reasons to keep us out of Heaven; He's looking for reasons to let us in!

No description of love anywhere in the literature of mankind surpasses that given by the apostle Paul in the 13th chapter of First Corinthians. *The Amplified Bible* gives us shades of meaning from the Greek that do not directly translate into English.

> *Love endures long and is patient and kind; love never is envious nor boils over with jealousy, is not boastful or vainglorious, does not display itself haughtily. It is not conceited (arrogant and inflated with pride); it is not rude (unmannerly) and does not act unbecomingly. Love (God's love in us) does not insist on its own rights or its own way, for it is not self-seeking; it is not touchy or fretful or resentful;*

it takes no account of the evil done to it [it pays no attention to a suffered wrong]. It does not rejoice at injustice and unrighteousness, but rejoices when right and truth prevail. Love bears up under anything and everything that comes, is ever ready to believe the best of every person, its hopes are fadeless under all circumstances, and it endures every thing [without weakening]. Love never fails [never fades out or becomes obsolete or comes to an end] (1 Corinthians 13:4-8a, AMP).

The kind of love Paul is talking about has its source in God and comes only from Him. Since God is love, whatever the Bible says about love is also true of God. Substituting God's name for the word "love" reveals the meaning of this passage in a new light:

God is patient, God is kind. God does not envy, God does not boast, God is not proud. God is not rude, God is not self-seeking, God is not easily angered, God keeps no record of wrongs. God does not delight in evil but rejoices with the truth. God always protects, always trusts, always hopes, always perseveres. God never fails (1 Corinthians 13:4-8a, NIV).

That's quite a different picture of God from what the world paints, isn't it? All of this applies equally to Jesus Christ because He is of the same essence as God the Father. In fact, Jesus Himself said, "I and the Father are one" (Jn. 10:30). Jesus loves us. He proved it when He went willingly to the cross to die in our place so we could be forgiven and made right with God.

"Jesus Loves Me": So Simple, It's Hard

SOMETIMES THE SIMPLEST TRUTHS are the most difficult to grasp because we have a tendency to make things more complicated than they need to be. That's one reason why Jesus said, "I tell you the truth, anyone who will not receive the kingdom of God like a little child will never enter it" (Lk. 18:17). The simple, trusting, loving faith of a child is our example. When children believe God, they simply take Him at His word. We should do the same.

One of the hardest things for many Christians to truly understand and personally believe is the simple yet profound truth contained in the words, "Jesus loves me." After all, how is that possible? It seems too easy, too fantastic, too good to be true. Although we may not have much trouble accepting the idea of Jesus' love for mankind overall, believing He loves each of us *personally* is another story.

The Lord does not love us in bunches, like bananas, but individually. Jesus loves me *individually*, and He loves you *individually*. "But Mike, you don't know what I've done. You don't know how I've let the Lord down!" You're right. I *don't* know, but that doesn't matter. What matters is that Jesus knows—*and He loves you anyway*. "But Mike, everybody is telling me that I'm finished; that I've screwed up too badly to ever be of use to the Lord again. How can He still love me?" Don't worry about what others say. Their opinions don't matter because it is not up to them. What matters is God's opinion, which is revealed in the words, "I have loved you with an everlasting love; I have drawn you with loving-kindness" (Jer. 31:3b). No matter who we are, what we've done, where we've been, or how badly we've messed up, God's love for us never changes.

"Jesus loves me." No truth on earth is more profound than this, and yet it is so simple that even a child can understand it. Maybe that is why Anna B. Warner's hymn remains so popular well over a century after she wrote it:

Jesus loves me! This I know, For the Bible tells me
  so;
Little ones to Him belong; They are weak but He is
  strong.
Yes, Jesus loves me, Yes, Jesus loves me,
Yes, Jesus loves me, The Bible tells me so.

It's really a shame that so many Christians write off that hymn as a "children's song" and never give serious thought to what it says. The implications of those simple words are truly breathtaking. They speak to the very heart and nature of who God is.

Think about it for a minute. Make it personal. Jesus loves *you*. He who is the King of kings and the Lord of lords loves *you*. He whom the Bible calls the lily of the valley, the bright and morning star, and the fairest of ten thousand, loves *you*. He who knew you before you were formed in your mother's womb, who knows the number of every hair on your head, and who has your name carved into the palm of His hand, loves *you*.

The One who put the stars in the night sky, through whom all things were created and without whom nothing was created, loves *you*. He who could gather His entire creation into the palm of one hand and drop it in His eye without even blinking, loves *you*. Almighty God, the Three-in-One, Father, Son, and Holy Spirit, loves *you*. If that thought doesn't take your breath away, maybe you need to check to make sure you're still alive!

As Christians we are members of a new covenant with God that was signed, sealed, and delivered by the blood of Christ. The Bible is the written record of that covenant, and it plainly states that God loves us totally, unequivocally, and unconditionally.

One of the reasons we sometimes have difficulty believing that Jesus really loves us is because we focus on our

41

unworthiness rather than on God's willingness. We look at our own weaknesses and failures and wonder how in the world *anyone* could love such a mess. God's love for us is based not on our worthiness but on His grace. That's why we can never do anything to make God stop loving us.

Jerry Bridges, in his book *The Practice of Godliness*, writes:

> ...we must realize that [God's] love is *entirely of grace*, that it rests completely upon the work of Jesus Christ and flows to us through our union with Him. Because of this basis His love can never change, regardless of what we do. In our daily experience, we have all sorts of spiritual ups and downs—sin, failure, discouragement, all of which tend to make us question God's love. That is because we keep thinking that God's love is somehow conditional. We are afraid to believe His love is based entirely upon the finished work of Christ for us.
>
> Deep down in our souls we must get hold of the wonderful truth that our spiritual failures do not affect God's love for us one iota—that His love for us does not fluctuate according to our experience. We must be gripped by the truth that we are accepted by God and loved by God for the sole reason that we are united to His beloved Son.[1]

It is because of this unshakeable foundation of Christ's finished work for us that Paul was able to state with such confidence, "For I am convinced that neither death nor life, neither angels nor demons, neither the present nor the future, nor any powers, neither height nor depth, nor anything else in all creation, will be able to separate us from the love of God that is in Christ Jesus our Lord" (Rom. 8:38-39).

Jesus loves you! Don't make that harder than it is; just accept it. Relax and rejoice in the assurance that you are deeply loved, completely forgiven, fully pleasing, totally accepted by God, and absolutely complete in Christ!

Watch Out for the Rake!

WHEN YOU GET RIGHT DOWN TO IT, the only sure thing we have in life is the love of Jesus. No matter how thoroughly we try to prepare ourselves for the ups and downs and challenges of daily living, there will always be something that somewhere, sometime catches us unawares. You may feel like you can take on the whole world. You've got your pith helmet on so the sun won't shine on you, and you wear a mosquito net so you won't get bitten by anything nasty. You've got your gloves on, and your heavy long-sleeved shirt, long trousers, and waterproof and snake-proof boots. Now you're ready to walk through the garden of life completely prepared for anything. You march out with a confident swagger... and that's when you step on the rake. *Whacko!* —and you're down for the count.

It's always the unexpected—the stuff we're *not* prepared for—that knocks our brains out. We sit on the ground seeing stars, shaking our heads, and wondering what hit us. Let's face it, sometimes adversity strikes us like an artillery barrage and leaves us battered, bruised, bleeding, and wandering around the cratered battlefield in a shell-shocked daze. Whether the bombardment comes from the enemy, from our own foolishness, or from some angry or disgruntled brothers or sisters in Christ, the wreckage can be devastating. Surrounded by the debris of everything we thought we could count on, we discover that the only thing we have to hold on to is the love of Jesus.

There's nothing like a little disaster in life to make you see clearly what is truly important. When my world fell apart in 1992, the only thing that kept me going was the knowledge in my spirit that Jesus loved me. Soon I began to realize that as long as I had the love of Jesus, nothing else really mattered. In Him I had all I needed. Everything else was just stuff and fluff.

The apostle Paul discovered this in his own experience. That's why he was able to say, "But whatever was to my profit I now consider loss for the sake of Christ. What is more, I consider everything a loss compared to the surpassing greatness of knowing Christ Jesus my Lord, for whose sake I have lost all things" (Phil. 3:7-8a), and "...I have learned to be content whatever the circumstances" (Phil. 4:11b). Because Paul's anchor was in Christ, the ups and downs of life could not shake him. Because he valued the love of Christ above all else, the things of the world held no allure for him.

Getting hit by "friendly fire" is a lot like finding the rake in the yard the hard way. It hurts so much because it is totally unexpected. What's worse is looking around after your head has cleared a little bit, finding yourself all alone, and realizing that no one has come back to pick you up. At times like that it is so important to be able to fall back on the certain truth of the love of Christ. Even if everyone else forsakes you, He never will. As the writer of Hebrews points out, "God has said, 'Never will I leave you; never will I forsake you' " (Heb. 13:5b).

God Is Always in the Lost-and-Found Business

THE 15TH CHAPTER OF LUKE RECORDS three of Jesus' most well-known parables: the lost sheep, the lost coin, and the lost son. These stories comprise a trilogy on the theme of the persistent and seeking love of God. In the first (see Lk. 15:1-7), the shepherd leaves 99 sheep safely in the fold while he hunts diligently for one sheep that is lost. Upon finding it, he brings it home and throws a big party to celebrate. The second parable (see Lk. 15:8-10) tells of a woman with ten gold coins who, losing one, searches her house from top to bottom until she finds it. She too invites some friends to rejoice with her.

Jesus then relates the story of a father and his two sons, the younger of whom insists on receiving his inheritance early so he can enjoy it immediately. (Today, we call that "instant gratification.") Money in hand, the young man goes away to a far country where he quickly wastes his substance in wild living. Reduced to hiring himself out to feed pigs (what self-respecting Jewish boy would ever do that!), he eventually comes to his senses and decides to return home. Hoping for nothing more than to be received as a servant, this wayward son rehearses in his mind what he will say to his father. This is where the central thrust of the story comes in.

> *So he got up and went to his father. But while he was still a long way off, his father saw him and was filled with compassion for him; he ran to his son, threw his arms around him and kissed him. The son said to him, "Father, I have sinned against heaven and against you. I am no longer worthy to be called your son." But the father said to his servants, "Quick! Bring the best robe and put it on him. Put a ring on his finger and sandals on his feet. Bring the fattened calf and kill it. Let's have a feast and celebrate. For this son of mine was dead and is alive again; he was lost and is found." So they began to celebrate* (Luke 15:20-24).

These three related parables are traditionally (and rightly) understood as pertaining to conversion and the importance of each individual relationship with God. I believe there is another meaning as well. Aside from focusing on redemption, these stories illustrate *restoration*. After all, the lost sheep was originally part of the flock, but wandered away; the shepherd found it and *restored* it to the fold. Likewise, the woman found the lost coin and *restored* it to its proper place with the others. Although the father did not go after his wayward son, he fervently desired and actively watched for his return. That's why he saw his son "while he was still a long way off," and ran to embrace him. The son knew he deserved nothing better than to be one of his father's hired servants (if that!), yet the father *restored* his son to his original status in the family.

Jesus' picture of this loving father is particularly vivid because in the culture of that day, such a flagrantly public display of emotion as that shown by the father would have been regarded as unseemly and undignified for someone of his age and status in the community. The father's love and compassion for his son and his joy over the young man's return overrode any concern he may have had for accepted standards of social decorum. His errant son, whom he loved with all his heart, had come home. Nothing else mattered.

Such is the extravagant nature of God's love for us. He is always seeking, always longing for us to come home. Whether we are lost and need to be saved, or whether we are saved but need to be restored, if we repent and turn to the Lord, He will rush to embrace us with open arms of everlasting love.

The cross of Christ is the key. Jesus proved His love on Calvary. Not only does the cross demonstrate God's love for us, it also makes His love accessible to us and active in our lives. Since the basis of our relationship with God is neither our behavior nor our worthiness, but the finished work of Christ, nothing we do or do not do will ever change God's love, grace, and mercy toward us.

If you're beaten down because you feel you have betrayed the Lord; if you're afraid you're too messed up to ever come back; if others in the Body of Christ have dumped on you because of your failures; take heart: *Jesus loves you!* No matter where you are right now and no matter what has happened, like the father in the parable, Jesus stands watching for you, waiting for you to return to Him so He can *restore* you. Like the prodigal son who came to his senses while squatting in the pigsty, the decision is yours. The only one who can prevent you from being restored is *you*. Come back to Jesus. He loves you and He will never turn you away.

How much does the Lord love us? Consider the words of this prayer by Catherine of Siena, a 14th-century Italian mystic and influential church leader:

> Dear Lord, it seems that you are so madly in love with your creatures that you could not live without us. So you created us; and then, when we turned away from you, you redeemed us. Yet you are God, and so have no need of us. Your greatness is made no greater by our creation; your power is made no stronger by our redemption. You have no duty to care for us, no debt to repay us. It is love, and love alone, which moves you.

ENDNOTE

1. Jerry Bridges, *The Practice of Godliness* (Colorado Springs, CO: NavPress Publishing Group, 1983, 1996), 26-27.

Chapter Three

You *Can* Survive the Church

When you take a licking, keep on ticking.

I HAVE A PREACHER FRIEND whose wife left him after carrying on an extramarital affair for three years with an underaged boy. My friend was willing to go to counseling or to do anything else that was necessary in order to save his marriage. He truly wanted to reconcile with his wife, but despite all his efforts, she divorced him anyway. Not long after this, his denomination stripped him of his preaching credentials. According to their rules, no one who had been through a divorce could hold clerical papers in that denomination.

Undoubtedly, such a rule existed for good reason: to prevent anyone involved in sexual immorality from occupying a pulpit. Not only is that a wise precaution, it is certainly biblical. In my friend's case, however, strict adherence to the letter of the law led his denomination to punish him for something that somebody else did. Although my friend did nothing wrong and was never personally involved in any immorality, they took away his freedom and ability to minister and fulfill God's calling on his life.

At no time was any attempt made to help him, to restore him, to save his ministry, or even simply to stand by him while he went through the most gut-wrenching experience of his life. Basically, he was abandoned and left hanging to twist slowly in the wind.

Fortunately for my friend, however, a group of people from the grassroots level and from outside denominational lines rallied around him—people who knew him, loved him, believed in him, grieved with him, and supported him. It was not just the "slap-on-the-back-don't-worry-you-did-everything-right" kind of support, but the kind where they loved him, stood by him, and helped him face up to the truth about his responsibility, yet without judging him. Because of their love and support, my friend was restored. Today he is pastoring again, in an independent work.

Sadly, my friend's experience is neither unique nor uncommon. Thousands of believers could tell similar stories of being on the receiving end of a legalistic bludgeoning at the hands of others in the Church. More often than not, these actions are taken for the sake of "doctrinal integrity," "theological correctness," or even "faithfulness to the Word of God." At least, those are the reasons given. The problem is that whether or not those reasons are well-grounded, it is very easy to cross the line between integrity and extremism. When that happens, any spirit of the love and compassion of Christ is lost, a precious brother or sister is deeply wounded, and the entire Church suffers.

Legalism and license are two extremes that are equally dangerous to the life and health of the Body of Christ. Rigid adherence to the "letter of the law" that is devoid of love and compassion leads to a "religion" that is formal, cold, austere, joyless, and unforgiving. At the other end of the spectrum, love and compassion that de-emphasizes the moral and spiritual standards of God's Word can result in an "anything goes" attitude.

These extremes can occur whenever there is an imbalance between the *ekklesia* and the *koinonia*—between the *institutional structure* of the church and the *fellowship* of the Body.

Relationships Help Us Survive Religion

EKKLESIA IS THE NEW TESTAMENT GREEK WORD for "church." It literally means "assembly," or "called-out ones." For our purposes here, I am using *ekklesia* to mean the *institution* of the church—its formal, organized framework. The *ekklesia* is the "skeleton" of the body, the ecclesiastical structure of the church with all its traditions and governing rules and regulations. Within this context, *ekklesia* also refers to the congregation of the "religious": the self-appointed, self-righteous ones who judge all other believers by their own particular (and often peculiar) standards of holiness and spirituality.

If *ekklesia* is the "skeleton" of the church, then *koinonia* is its *heart*. The Greek word *koinonia* literally means "partnership" or "participation," but is most often translated "fellowship." It refers specifically to the fellowship of believers, the spiritual communion that Christians have with Christ and with one another. *Ekklesia* focuses on religion, while *koinonia* centers around relationships. *Koinonia* is essential for balance with *ekklesia*. We all need relationships in order to survive religion.

My preacher friend survived and was restored because he found *koinonia* in a group of fellow believers with whom he had ongoing relationships. Otherwise, the *ekklesia* of his denomination alone would have destroyed him.

51

One thing I discovered through my own experience is that during painful times you find out very quickly who your true friends are. A lot of people I thought were my friends turned out not to be. A handful of others—my true friends—rallied around me, lifted me up, and stayed with me through the worst time of my life. Among these were some new folks who appeared during my ordeal and quickly became lasting friends. From that nucleus a wider network of friends has grown up over the years so that now my ministry is based primarily on the relationships I have developed.

For most of us, the number of true brothers and sisters in Christ we have—people we develop deep relationships with—will be relatively small. They are the ones from whom we will draw our real strength and encouragement. They are the ones in whom we will see a true picture of Christ and know what He is really like. Jesus will manifest Himself in the flesh to us through our friends, and *through* us *to* our friends. That is the heart and soul of *koinonia*.

Kept in balance, the structure of *ekklesia* is necessary because it brings order and stability; it is a means to an end. Problems arise when that structure becomes an end in itself, existing for its own sake. One symptom of this is when perpetuation of the structure becomes the primary concern while the needs and hearts of people occupy a secondary place. Whenever the needs of the structure outweigh the needs of the people, *ekklesia* becomes toxic.

Another sign that *ekklesia* is out of balance in a church is the practice of vain observance. Vain observance is an action performed for its own sake long after the reason for it has been forgotten. The best example I have ever heard came from a buddy of mine. While on a trip to Germany he visited a Lutheran church where he witnessed an unusual practice. As the parishioners entered the sanctuary, they each patted a particular spot on the wall as they passed. Curious, my friend asked one of the elders, "Why do you pat the wall when you come in?" The elder answered, "I don't really know. We have always patted the wall. Our fathers did it, and so did our grandfathers and our great grandfathers."

After digging around in the historical records, they discovered that four hundred years earlier, before the Reformation, the church had been a Catholic church. On the wall inside the door had been a picture of the Blessed Virgin Mary, and as the people entered, they would put their hand on the picture and pray, "Bless me." For centuries that picture had been covered over, yet the congregation, good Lutherans though they were, still patted the wall in that same spot. It was a gesture without meaning—a vain observance.

Don't Be Fooled by False Holiness

GOD HAS NEVER BEEN INTERESTED in "religious" observances for their own sake; His heart has always longed for relationships with people. We all have a tendency, however, to substitute ritual for relationship and tradition for genuine worship. This is not a new problem. Jesus confronted it often in His encounters with the Pharisees and other Jewish religious leaders of His day. Once, when the Pharisees challenged Jesus and His disciples over their failure to observe the "traditions of the elders" because they did not wash their hands before eating, Jesus charged His critics with violating the commands of God for the sake of their tradition. Then, quoting from Isaiah, Jesus laid it on the line:

> *You hypocrites! Isaiah was right when he prophe-*
> *sied about you: "These people honor Me with their*

lips, but their hearts are far from Me. They worship Me in vain; their teachings are but rules taught by men" (Matthew 15:7-9).

The Lord wants our heart affection, not our vain observance of man-made rules or outmoded tradition. Unfortunately, many believers have been battered senseless from running headlong into a solid wall of religious legalism. An out-of-control *ekklesia* is beating them to death. Pharisaism is alive and well in many churches and prevents countless believers from experiencing the full *koinonia* they so desperately need.

One of the best illustrations of the contrast between *ekklesia* and *koinonia*—between ritual and relationship—is found in Jesus' parable about the Pharisee and the tax collector.

Two men went up to the temple to pray, one a Pharisee and the other a tax collector. The Pharisee stood up and prayed about himself: "God, I thank You that I am not like other men—robbers, evildoers, adulterers—or even like this tax collector. I fast twice a week and give a tenth of all I get." But the tax collector stood at a distance. He would not even look up to heaven, but beat his breast and said, "God, have mercy on me, a sinner." I tell you that this man, rather than the other, went home justified before God. For everyone who exalts himself will be humbled, and he who humbles himself will be exalted (Luke 18:10-14).

The Pharisee was not concerned about a personal relationship with God; he was too busy crossing his "t's" and dotting his "i's." Institutional religion was the focus of his life. In his eyes, that *was* the relationship. The tax collector, on the other hand, cut right to the chase. External religious trappings meant nothing to him; he was a sinner in need of forgiveness. Ignoring the institution, he looked beyond the law, appealed directly to God's mercy, and found God waiting to receive him with open arms. Where the unyielding *ekklesia* of the Pharisee would have destroyed him, the tax collector looked to the *koinonia* of God and found life and peace.

The tax collector was justified not because he was a sinner but because he repented. The Pharisee was condemned not because he fasted, tithed, and lived a moral life but because he condemned another. It is not hypocritical to try to live a Christian life; it is hypocritical to condemn those who can't.

Pharisees live for the *ekklesia*. They thrive on its rules and regulations and on the superiority they feel over others who are not as scrupulous as they are. Thomas Merton once said that a pharisee is a "righteous" man whose "righteousness" is nourished by the blood of sinners. They are the people who are hypocritically self-righteous and judgmental and who judge others according to their own personal standards of holiness. Wise and righteous in their own eyes, they set themselves up as judge and jury for everybody else.

In their minds holiness equates to outward appearances. Get your hair cut and you'll be a little more holy. Dress in the "right" kind of clothes and you'll be holier still. The more rules you keep and the more religious you act the holier you are. People with this kind of mind-set tend to be harshly judgmental because they are working so hard on their own personal holiness and feel threatened whenever somebody else doesn't see things the way they do.

True holiness is a work of the Spirit of God that begins in our hearts and then manifests itself in our outward behavior. It differs from false holiness in source, motivation, and focus. False holiness is centered on man, motivated by pride, and focused on self-advancement and earning God's favor. True holiness has its source in God, is motivated by love, and focused on becoming like Jesus.

The *ekklesia* promotes false holiness because it centers on *law*; the *koinonia* encourages true holiness because it centers on *grace*. Law locks us into trying to earn God's favor through our own human efforts. This is futile because Scripture plainly states that "no one will be declared righteous in [God's] sight by observing the law" (Rom. 3:20a). The purpose of the law is to make us aware of our sinfulness. Grace, on the other hand, sets us free because it shows us that in Christ we already have God's favor as a free gift:

> *This righteousness from God comes through faith in Jesus Christ to all who believe. There is no difference, for all have sinned and fall short of the glory of God, and are justified freely by His grace through the redemption that came by Christ Jesus* (Romans 3:22-24).

> *For it is by grace you have been saved, through faith—and this not from yourselves, it is the gift of God—not by works, so that no one can boast* (Ephesians 2:8-9).

Don't be fooled by false holiness. God's grace has set you free in Christ. *No one* has the right to hold you to a false standard of behavior or godliness that is according to their own design. God's standard is the only one that matters, and He has said, "I love you. You are Mine. Through the blood of My Son you are fully accepted."

Shake It Off and Step Up

SO WHAT DO YOU DO when you're being pelted with the stones of someone else's negative criticism or unjustified demands or expectations? How do you weather the bombardment of the *ekklesia*? It's not always easy, but one key is to learn to "shake it off and step up."

Once there was a farmer who owned an old mule. One day, because of failing eyesight, the mule stumbled into the farmer's well. Immediately he began braying desperately for help. Hearing the animal's cries, the farmer quickly assessed the situation and decided that, even though he felt sympathy for the old mule, neither he nor the well was worth the trouble of saving. Instead, he called some of his neighbors together, explained the situation, and enlisted their help in hauling dirt to fill in the well, thereby burying the mule and putting him out of his misery.

At first the old mule panicked. Each shovelful of dirt hitting his back seemed to spell certain doom. Then a sudden spark of inspiration lit up his mulish brain. Whenever a load of dirt landed on his back, all he had to do was *shake it off and step up*! This he did, shovelful after shovelful. Shake it off and step up...shake it off and step up...shake it off and step up. No matter how painful the blows or how distressing the situation became, that old mule fought off his panic and just kept shaking it off and stepping up.

After awhile, that old mule, battered and exhausted, stepped triumphantly over the wall of that well. That which otherwise would have buried him became blessings for him, all because of the way he handled his adversity.

Life is like that sometimes. Our adversity can either bury us or bless us, depending on our attitude. If we face our problems, our difficulties, and the criticisms of others in a positive way, without giving in to panic, bitterness, or self-pity, we can turn those bombs into blessings. Often we cannot control either the troubles that come our way or the critical or judgmental words of others about us, but we can control how we respond to them. None of the jabs, barbs, or mud thrown at us by others can stick unless we allow it.

Just "shake it off and step up." Let your adversities become stepping-stones to building character and drawing closer to the Lord. Forgiveness, faith, prayer, praise, and hope are all excellent ways to "shake it off and step up" out of the wells we find ourselves in (or that others throw us into).

It's Always Darkest Before the Dawn

ONE OF THE CLASSIC STRATEGIES in warfare is for an attacking army to "soften up" a well-entrenched enemy by hitting them with extensive bombing and artillery barrages before sending in ground troops. The purpose behind this is to demoralize the enemy by raining death and destruction on them, keep them hunkered down under cover, wear them to a nervous frazzle, and generally destroy their will to resist. Well-trained and well-seasoned troops know that if they persevere under attack—if they hold without breaking—they may still carry the day. If at some point during the onslaught they decide they cannot hang on, then the battle is over.

Perseverance is just as important for us as believers whenever we are trying to survive "friendly fire" from others in the Body of Christ. Those experiences often are the darkest days of our lives. The problem with dark days is that while we are going through them we rarely know how long they will last or how near or far we are from the end. From the standpoint of darkness, there is little difference between midnight and 5 a.m. At midnight a full night of darkness looms ahead, but at 5 a.m. dawn is just around the corner. There's a lot of truth in the old saying, "It's always darkest before the dawn." We may be going through the deepest darkness of our life, but for all we know, the light may be approaching fast.

What's my point? Whatever you do, *don't give up*. No matter how tough things get or how much you hurt, *don't drop out*. One of satan's most effective strategies is to rob us of victory, not early on when we have just begun to fight, but at the 11th hour when the end of our struggle is in sight. That's when he jumps in and tries to cut us off at the knees. It's hard to keep trying after we've had victory snatched from our fingers at the last minute.

There's an old Easter sermon called "It's Friday, but Sunday's Coming!" Jesus died on Friday but don't worry, Sunday's coming. Things may be dark now but don't worry, Sunday's coming. Death may be all around but don't worry, Sunday's coming. So hang in there! Don't give up. No matter how dark the night, it is only temporary. Dawn is coming soon.

Winston Churchill, speaking to an assembly of students during some of England's darkest days during World War II, encouraged his young audience to persevere: "Never give in, never give in, never, never, never, never—in nothing, great or small, large or petty—never give in except to convictions of honor and good sense."[1] That pretty much says it.

Just as light and darkness are *both* part of God's design in creation, sunny days and dark nights of the soul are both part of life. Dark times are necessary because they build character and help bring us to maturity both in life and in ministry. The secret is to *stand*, no matter what. That's what the apostle Paul was getting at when he wrote, "Finally, be strong in the Lord and in His mighty power. Put on the full armor of God so that you can take your stand against the devil's schemes.... Therefore put on the full armor of God, so that when the day of evil comes, you may be able to stand your ground, and after you have done everything, to stand" (Eph. 6:10-11,13) and,

"Let us not become weary in doing good, for at the proper time we will reap a harvest if we do not give up" (Gal. 6:9).

King David of Israel was no stranger to difficult times. In fact, he could be the poster child for dark seasons of the soul. His is the voice of firsthand experience:

> I will exalt You, O Lord, for You lifted me out of the depths and did not let my enemies gloat over me. O Lord my God, I called to You for help and You healed me. O Lord, You brought me up from the grave; You spared me from going down into the pit. Sing to the Lord, you saints of His; praise His holy name. For His anger lasts only a moment, but His favor lasts a lifetime; weeping may remain for a night, but rejoicing comes in the morning (Psalm 30:1-5).

So what does it mean to persevere? It means going to church even when you don't feel like it. It means reading the Bible even when you don't feel like it. It means praying even when you don't feel like it. It means praising and worshiping God even when you don't feel like it.

All of us go through dry seasons, those times when it seems as though God doesn't even see us. You're down and depressed and nothing seems to work. No prayer gets past your hat, you can't get into the Word, and everything just seems out of kilter. The very idea of singing praise to the Lord makes you want to puke, and you've decided that if one more person comes up to you and says something "spiritual," you're going to punch them right in the teeth. Have you ever felt like that? I know I have.

Those are the times when it is the most important of all to stay focused and engaged. Draw near to the Lord. Lean on the Holy Spirit for wisdom, guidance, and the strength to stand. Many folks look to the Holy Spirit for flashy manifestations and gifts. Those are okay as far as they go, but they are not the real heart of the matter. When we learn to yield and depend on the Holy Spirit, one of the main things He imparts to us is the ability to persevere through times of hardship. Jesus said, "I have told you these things, so that in Me you may have peace. In this world you will have trouble. But take heart! I have overcome the world" (Jn. 16:33). As Paul wrote to the Romans, "If God is for us, who can be against us?" (Rom. 8:31b) Who indeed?

Find some fellow believers with whom you can build *koinonia*—people you can fellowship with and confide in, who will support you and lift you up and for whom you can do the same. At the same time, learn when and how to keep your own counsel. Use discretion and pray for discernment. Not everyone needs to know about your troubles. Some people can't be trusted with the secrets of your heart.

Lions and Tigers and Bears, Oh My!

ONE OF THE BIGGEST BATTLES in recovering from the effects of "friendly fire" is the battle within our own minds. First of all, it is so easy to fixate on our pain, our hurt, our anger, our bitterness, our disillusionment, or our guilt to the point that we lose all sense of perspective. Our problems swell up so big in our minds that there is no room to consider solutions. Fear is another factor that can hold us back: fear of being wounded again, fear of failure, fear of discovering that our attackers may be right after all and that we really have screwed up and made ourselves useless to everyone, God included.

Second, we humans have a strange tendency to start believing what others say about us, whether good or bad, if we hear it often enough. It only takes two or three different peo-ple to remark that we don't look well before we're convinced that we're sick. Part of our mental battle is to keep a balanced perspective. Our problems are almost never as big as we make them out to be in our minds. Learning to concentrate on the *solution* rather than the problem will help keep our fears and troubles from overwhelming us. Keeping our eyes on the goal will help us finish the race.

In *The Wizard of Oz*, Dorothy, the Scarecrow, and the Tin Woodsman have to cross through a forest on their way to the Emerald City. Hearing that the forest is full of scary creatures they enter timidly, trying to bolster their courage by chanting, "Lions and tigers and bears, oh my!...Lions and tigers and bears, oh my!" A few minutes later the Cowardly Lion leaps out at them in a display of false ferocity. After an initial fright, Dorothy, the Scarecrow, and the Tin Woodsman discover that the Lion is all bluff and bluster. Their fear was unfounded; the trouble they anticipated proved to be much less than they imagined.

That's the way it is with us in life. We allow our problems to swell much bigger than they really are and crowd out our view of the goal. In *The Wizard of Oz*, the goal was the Emer-ald City, not the frightening animals in the forest. The "lions and tigers and bears" were only a distraction.

Keeping our eyes on the prize is a biblical principle of spiritual growth. The apostle Paul knew this, which is why he wrote, "But one thing I do: Forgetting what is behind and strain-ing toward what is ahead, I press on toward the goal to win the prize for which God has called me heavenward in Christ Jesus" (Phil. 3:13b-14). The writer of Hebrews makes the same point: "Therefore, since we are surrounded by such a great cloud of witnesses, let us throw off everything that hinders and the sin that so easily entangles, and let us run with perseverance the race marked out for us. Let us fix our eyes on Jesus, the author and perfecter of our faith…" (Heb. 12:1-2a).

That's the key: *fixing our eyes on Jesus*. Sometimes it is a real battle to keep our minds focused on the Lord. When your child is lying in the hospital sick, it's hard to keep your eyes fixed on Jesus. If you've just lost your husband or your wife in a car accident, it's hard to keep your eyes fixed on Jesus. If you just got wiped out financially, it's hard to keep your eyes fixed on Jesus. If some brothers or sisters in Christ have bashed you because you failed or because you don't conform to their standards, it's hard to keep your eyes fixed on Jesus. But if you focus on your problems they will eat your lunch; they will suck you right down into a pit of despair that you may never climb out of.

Romans 11:29 says, "For the gifts and calling of God are without repentance" (KJV). No matter what you have done, no matter where you are right now in your walk with Christ, no matter how low you have fallen (or think you have fallen), God has not revoked His calling on your life or retracted the spiritual gifts He gave you when you became a Christian. No one on earth has the right to deny you the opportunity to become the full person God created you to be. No one on earth has the right to prevent you from fulfilling your potential and realizing God's purpose for your life.

Don't worry about what happened in the past. Don't allow the opinions of others to determine your future. Don't let the oppression of the *ekklesia* separate you from the *koinonia* of Christ. Fix your eyes on Jesus and trust Him to lead you, heal you, and restore you. Believe it or not, you *can* survive the church!

Let the words of this 8th-century Irish prayer encourage you:

Be Thou my vision,
O Lord of my heart.
Be all else but Naught to me,
Save that Thou art.
Be Thou my best thought
In the day and the night;
Both waking and sleeping,
Thy presence my light.

ENDNOTE

1. Winston Churchill, quoted in *Bartlett's Familiar Quotations, 16th ed.* by John Bartlett, Justin Kaplan, ed. (New York: Little, Brown and Co., 1992), 621:5.

Chapter Four

WHO SAYS YOU'RE FINISHED?

Depth of mercy! Can there be
Mercy still reserved for me?
—*Charles Wesley*

IN THE WEEKS FOLLOWING the collapse of
my ministry in late 1992 and early 1993 I reached the point
where I thought I was finished. How could I possibly go on
after what had happened? One morning I was lying on the
floor praying, "God, give me a job, because I need to pay my
bills." As far as I was concerned, it was all over for me. Continuing on in the ministry was out of the question. It was never
a matter of whether or not I was going to keep serving the
Lord—that was a given. I was smart enough to realize that I
could serve the Lord simply by mowing grass at the church. I
had given my life to Jesus and had determined to serve Him
until I died or He returned, whichever came first. I knew I
could never *not* serve the Lord.

Maybe I could be an associate pastor or a minister of
education at a church somewhere. Perhaps I could teach
school. Something—*anything*. As I lay on the floor telling
God how much I needed a job, I heard Him speak to me. I've

only heard the audible voice of God twice in my life, and this was one of them. If anyone else had been present, I don't know if they would have heard anything or not, but I did. The Lord said to me very clearly, "I *gave* you a job; get up off the floor."

I may have thought I was through, but God didn't. At that moment I knew beyond a doubt that His call to be an evangelist and minister of the gospel of Jesus Christ—the same call He had given me over 20 years earlier—was still valid. That part of my life had not changed. My ministry was in shambles, the business empire I had built as the number-one Christian comedian in America lay in pieces at my feet, and my witness for Christ had been publicly disgraced, but His call remained.

There was nothing to do but pick myself up and start over. At that point I had nothing left but the love of Jesus and the certainty of my call. The road to restoration was long and hard and required a lot of patience and humility. Part of that process involved voluntarily placing myself under submission to the authority of an oversight board made up of pastors who were willing to work with me and help me.

I Rebuilt My Ministry Through Relationships

ANOTHER PART OF MY RESTORATION was rebuilding my ministry by lining up places to preach. The only way to do that was to make cold contact calls to pastors asking for opportunities to speak and minister at their churches. It was a humbling experience. Can you imagine the humiliation, after 20 years of filling auditoriums around the world, of having to call and say, "Hi, this is Mike Warnke; could I come preach at your church?"

Sometimes I would call 15 people a day. In a typical response, three would say no while the other twelve would not even take my call. Generally, it went something like this:

"Hi. Could I please speak to Pastor Smith?"

"May I tell him who is calling?"

"This is Mike Warnke."

"Just a moment please." (Anxious pause) "I'm sorry, but the pastor is really busy right now. He'll have to call you back."

Sometimes I would get a call back, but not often. On those rare occasions when I was actually able to speak to a pastor, I usually heard different variations of the same theme: "Well, brother, I've heard some disturbing things about you and your ministry. Until all of that is cleared up, I don't think it would be a good idea for you to come."

This went on call after call, day after day. Finally, I would get one pastor who would say, "Sure, Brother Mike. Come on over. We'll be glad to help you out."

As exciting as it was to get a positive response, I had to accept the fact that some of these guys simply thought they were being kind to me by letting me come. They weren't necessarily super excited about having Mike Warnke in their church. It was not, "Oh good, we're going to have Brother Mike in our church, and he will really minister to our people" as much as it was, "Oh bless his little heart, we're going to do him a favor."

Don't get me wrong. I am very grateful to those pastors who were willing to take a chance with me, even while I was an "untouchable" in most Christian circles. In those early days of the controversy when I was just starting to get back on my feet, some of those pastors took a risk by letting me come, and I thank them for it.

Little by little, God opened doors and I began to preach again. Word of mouth helped a lot. One pastor would call a friend and say, "I just had Mike Warnke in my church, and he's doing pretty well. The anointing is still on him. As a matter of fact it's probably heavier now than it used to be. You ought to give him a shot." Then that same pastor would say to me, "Call this friend of mine. I've already spoken to him. Tell him who you are and that I recommended you." Slowly, by establishing a network of relationships like this, I was able to rebuild my ministry.

I am ministering now as much as I ever did, although not in the same circles or in the same way as before. Gone are the crowds of thousands in auditoriums and arenas. My ministry settings are much more intimate now: weekend conferences and Sunday worship services in churches with groups ranging in size from less than fifty up to several hundred. By the world's standards it is probably not the "successful" ministry it used to be, but it's not the world's standards that are important. God's standards are what counts. Today I am standing in the middle of my restoration because I am going where the Lord wants me to go and doing what the Lord wants me to do. Lost people are still getting saved and believers are rededicating their lives to the Lord. I couldn't be happier.

God Has Not Changed His Mind

MY EARLIER MINISTRY EXPLODED and went down in flames because I was out of order. I had built my "house" on sand instead of on rock. That failure, as spectacular and sudden as it was, did not mean that God had revoked or rescinded my calling. He was ready to restore me, but I had to be willing to be restored.

The Lord still loves us, even when we've messed up. He loves us when we're doing okay and when we're not. He loves us when we've got it all together and when we're scattered every which way. As Brennan Manning says, God loves us even when our cheese is falling off our cracker.

No matter what you may have done, no matter how brutally others in the Church have beaten up on you or shunned you or turned their back on you, no matter how badly you think you have failed the Lord, He has not changed His mind about you, and He never will. Romans 11:29 says, "For God's gifts and His call are irrevocable." That speaks plainly enough to me, but I like even better how the Amplified Bible states it:

> For God's gifts and His call are irrevocable. [He never withdraws them when once they are given, and He does not change His mind about those to whom He gives His grace or to whom He sends His call] (Rom. 11:29, AMP).

God doesn't love you when you do good and stop loving you when you do bad. He doesn't turn His back on you when you foul up. Some folks in the Body of Christ may do that, but the Lord doesn't. Even if you're a mess you still belong to the Lord. Even if you're in trouble, you still belong to the Lord. Even if you've made a huge and horrible mistake, you still belong to the Lord. He still loves you and He still has a plan for you. His calling on your life still stands, as sure and certain as ever. "A bruised reed He will not break, and a smoldering wick He will not snuff out" (Is. 42:3a).

Who says you're finished? No one on earth is in a position to judge you; only God has that authority. All of us are in the same boat: sinners standing in need of the Lord's grace, mercy, and forgiveness. Don't let the opinions or judgments of others press you down so you never get up again. God's opinion is the only one that matters. Paul put it this way:

> *What, then, shall we say in response to this? If God is for us, who can be against us? He who did not spare His own Son, but gave Him up for us all—how will He not also, along with Him, graciously give us all things? Who will bring any charge against those whom God has chosen? It is God who justifies* (Romans 8:31-33).

God's gifts and calling are irrevocable. Restoration is possible, but the Great Physician may have some medicine for you to take first. Have you repented for any sin on your part? Have you made amends or restitution, if necessary? Are you ready to follow God along whatever path He chooses for your restoration? It may not be pleasant at first, but just hold your nose and swallow your medicine.

My medicine was putting myself under authority. My medicine was not fighting back. My medicine was walking away from everything I had built and starting out from ground zero. My medicine was being Mike Warnke, yet humbling myself to call people and ask for opportunities to minister.

Your medicine won't be the same as mine, but it will be "just what the doctor ordered" for your particular situation. The Lord knows exactly what you need. He will provide it but only you can take it. Restoration is not automatic; you must take the initiative to follow God's lead.

The only one who could have kept Paul from getting up off the dusty Damascus road after being knocked off his horse by a vision of Christ was Paul himself (see Acts 9:1-19). God got Paul's attention, but Paul had to decide for himself to follow. The only one who could have kept Peter from going to the home of Cornelius after receiving a vision from God was Peter himself (see Acts 10). God told Peter what to do but it was up to Peter to obey. The only one who can keep you from going on with God after you've had a fall or made a big mistake is you. Trust God and take your medicine. Be patient. Give it time and it will heal you.

You Can Go on From Here

ONE IMPORTANT KEY TO SURVIVING "friendly fire" and getting on with your life is your own attitude. For example, you can think of the tough times as a crisis, or you can think of them as a period of adjustment in your life.

Generally speaking, there are two types of "friendly fire." The first is that which is completely unjust and undeserved, when we are accused of things we did not do and of saying things we did not say. People misunderstand us and misread our motives. They may feel like we've let them down because we did not live up to their expectations. This kind of criticism is probably the hardest to deal with.

The other kind of "friendly fire" is that which we bring upon ourselves because of our own mistakes. When other believers land on us hard because we really messed up, it can leave us feeling worthless, guilty, and fearful that God cannot or will not forgive us. What we may think of as "humility" is in reality extreme arrogance. After all, who are we to think that the love and mercy of God do not extend to us, or that our sins are so heinous that the blood of Jesus cannot wash them away?

The principal theme of the entire Bible is reconciliation and restoration. That which Adam and Eve lost in the opening chapters of Genesis—paradise and an intimate relationship with God—are fully restored in the closing chapters of Revelation. In between is the unfolding story of how God reconciled us to Himself and to that intimacy with Him that He always intended. The story of the Bible is the story of *koinonia* restored.

Take a look at King David, for example. Even though he is described as a man after God's own heart, he fell into great sin. Second Samuel chapters 11 and 12 describe David's descent into evil and his recovery from it. First, he lusted after another man's wife: Bathsheba, whose husband Uriah was one of David's bravest and most loyal generals. David's lust led to adultery, which led to illegitimate pregnancy, which led to a political cover-up, which led to Uriah's assassination. David seemed oblivious to the depth of his sin until Nathan, a prophet of the Lord, confronted him with it. His heart broken in sorrow and conviction, David confessed his sin before God, repented, and pleaded for forgiveness.

The Lord forgave David and restored him, but things were never exactly the same again. David was still king, he was still a man after God's own heart, and he still enjoyed the blessings of God on his life. Some things were different, however. The child conceived in David's adultery died, and for the rest of his life David endured turmoil, trouble, and even rebellion within his own house. Restoration does not always mean that we will regain everything we had before. It also does not mean that anyone who has had an indiscretion will necessarily lose a child. It does mean that God can use us in new and different ways in spite of our past failures.

Simon Peter is another good example. Despite all his boastful promises to the contrary, the big fisherman let Jesus down just when the Lord needed him most. When pressed by Jesus' enemies, three times Peter loudly declared, "I don't know Him!" The Bible says that as soon as the cock crowed and Peter realized what he had done, he went out and wept. I bet he bawled like a baby. I bet that at that moment Peter felt absolutely worthless, the lowest piece of slime on the planet, lower than the mud at the bottom of the Sea of Galilee.

The 21st chapter of John tells us that one day shortly after His resurrection, Jesus was on the shore near where Peter and six other disciples were fishing. When the men recognized Jesus, they hurried ashore. The boat was too slow for Peter, who jumped overboard and swam in. As the disciples shared breakfast with Jesus, He dealt directly with the terrible ache in Peter's heart. Three times (the same number of times Peter had denied knowing Him) Jesus asked, "Simon, do you love Me?" Each time Peter replied, "Yes, Lord, you know I love You." Then Jesus said, "Feed My sheep." Peter was restored. He still had fellowship with the Lord. He still had the call of Christ on his life to be a "fisher of men." He was humbler and wiser because of his failure, and that made him stronger.

Follow the Peace

WHEN YOU GET BURNED in ministry or bruised by other believers, a common reaction is to doubt your calling. It happens all the time. In the midst of discouragement and disillusionment, how can you be sure of your calling?

Once upon a time many years ago, I was living in Stillwater, Oklahoma and enrolled as a student at Trinity Bible College in Tulsa. At the same time I was traveling and preaching a lot. Trying to balance between school and my frequent travel started to get really crazy, so I decided to come off the road.

A friend of mine had just opened a small restaurant in Stillwater and needed someone to open up for him in the mornings and serve breakfast to the college students. The place was little more than a student dive, very small and casual, with the food served on paper plates. I told my friend that I'd be glad to take the job and work on the mornings I didn't have school, particularly on weekends.

On my very first morning, I went in, opened up, and got everything going. The first customer came in around 6:00 am. It was clear that this kid had just pulled an all-nighter and had wandered out to get a cup of coffee. He was all groggy and bleary-eyed, not functioning very well at all. He plopped down at the counter, looked at the menu, and said, "I want one egg." One of the items on the menu was a single egg: one egg with toast, or one egg with hash browns, or even one egg by itself.

"Okay," I said. "How do you want it?"

"Over easy."

Well, I slapped some grease in the skillet, put that baby on the grill and turned up the heat, slopped an egg in there and fried it up just as pretty as you please. Then I scooped it onto a paper plate and set it down in front of him. He just sat there staring at that egg in the center of that paper plate, and I just stood there staring at it with him. The grease was soaking right through the plate. Finally, the kid looked up at me and said, "I've got to get out of here."

I said, "Yeah, me too." I went over and turned everything off, hung up my apron, and he and I walked out. He left college and I called my buddy and said, "I'm not called to run your restaurant. I'm called to preach the gospel." And I went back on the road.

The only way I know of to be sure of your calling is when you cannot find any satisfaction doing anything else. Young people come up to me all the time and ask, "What do I need to do to get into the ministry like you?"

I tell them, "First, go home and pray about it for two years. After that, if you can do anything else at all, do it, because *if* you can do anything else at all, you're not called to do this. If you're called to do this, this is all you *can* do."

This doesn't mean there is nothing else you are capable of doing or trained to do, but there is nothing else you have an inner peace about doing. If the call of God is on your life in a particular area, you won't be satisfied doing anything else. There will be an internal fire, a deep inner drive that will not let you do anything else and find contentment or fulfillment in it.

When you are walking in your destiny and following God's plan for your life you will find an inner peace that cannot be found anywhere else. If you move away from that walk you will know it because the peace will depart. I've run across many guys who used to preach the gospel, but because of some mistake they've made, they no longer minister in the same capacity. They were called of God to preach the gospel but they're out selling cars or insurance or working in an office somewhere. They're the kind of guys who tend to talk a little too loudly or drink a little more coffee than they should or engage in a little more backslapping than is really necessary. This is their way of trying to convince you (as well as themselves) that they're okay and that what they are doing now is just as important and just as significant as what they used to do. Deep inside they know it's not true. They don't have the peace of being in God's will and so they try to compensate by an overdone display of enthusiasm.

So, my counsel to you is, *follow the peace*. That may sound ethereal or abstract, but it is the only reliable gauge I know. If your heart's desire is to do God's will and you are at peace with where you are and what you are doing, that's a good indication that you are where the Lord wants you. If you make a change and that peace doesn't follow you, then you can bet your bottom dollar that you are no longer in the will of God for your life.

Don't Judge by the World's Standards of Success

FOLLOWING THE PEACE INTO GOD'S WILL and walking the road to restoration does not necessarily mean that God will return you to where you were before or restore everything you once had. Fulfilling His purpose may take you in another direction. Success in God's Kingdom is finding out where God wants you to go and going there, and finding out what God wants you to do and doing it.

Somehow we've concocted the idea that the only way to really serve God is to be up in front of a lot of people talking about Jesus, or leading a big Bible study, or singing for a large audience, or something else flashy and splashy. That's the problem facing a lot of those guys (like me) who once had "big" and "important" ministries but lost them for any numbers of reasons. They assume that since they can't jump right back into something just as visible and prominent that God does not have anything else for them to do.

That's simply not true. If you are willing, God will make a way. My own experience is a perfect example. By outward appearances, my current ministry bears no resemblance to my previous one. During my 20 years as the number-one Christian comedian in America I regularly played to packed houses. Thousands attended my concerts and we routinely turned away several thousand more for lack of seats. Today, I minister in individual churches in much smaller and more intimate settings. Sometimes over a weekend I will meet with no more than one hundred people, and often fewer than that. Yet, I have a great sense of peace in what I am doing because I know

I am where God wants me. This *is* His will for me. I am no longer on the road to restoration; this *is* my restoration. I am standing in it.

My contentment and peace with my present less visible ministry has nothing to do with a feeling that I don't "deserve" anything better and should be happy with what I have. The truth is, I don't "deserve" to be able to serve God in *any* capacity. None of us do. It is only by His mercy and grace that any of us can serve Him and minister in His name. My peace comes from the knowledge—the rock-solid certainty—that I am walking in the center of God's will for my life. That is the true measure of success.

Many people who know and remember me from my earlier days have trouble understanding how I can be contented with where I am now. In their minds they still measure "success" in ministry as sellout crowds, best-selling books, tapes, and CDs, and multitudes responding to altar calls. I have a hard time convincing them that I truly am happy now and feel blessed to be able to minister to people the way I do.

Every now and then one of my old friends from those earlier days comes up to me and asks me about the change in my ministry. One of those conversations went something like this:

"Hey, Brother Mike, how are you doing?"

"Well, I'm doing just fine."

"No brother, really, *how are you doing*?"

"Really, I'm doing fine."

"How can you be doing fine? After all you had, and as far as you've fallen, you can't possibly be fine. You're just making the best of a bad situation."

Then I explained, "No brother, I'm fine. I haven't fallen from anything because I'm still in the will of God. This is the will of God for my life right now. As long as you are in the will of God, and as long as you are ministering according to what God is telling you to do, and as long as you are using the talents that God has given you to bless people, then you are as good as you need to be."

Unfortunately, many believers, especially those of us in the West, have the world's idea of success so deeply embedded in our minds and consciousness that we often measure a person's anointing by the size of his church, or by the number of people who attend her conference, or by how many books he has written, or by how many tapes and CDs she has sold, and so on.

In the world's eyes, Jesus Christ Himself was a failure during His lifetime. Don't judge yourself by the world's standards of success. What's important is meeting God's standards. Maybe you are going through a time of trial with the bombshells of "friendly fire" falling all around you. Maybe your ministry is changing in ways you never expected or desired. Be patient and don't despair. God may be preparing to bring you back to where you used to be, or He may have something completely different in mind. Whichever the case, keep in mind that He loves you and has your best interests at heart. His gifts and calling are irrevocable.

As long as you have life and breath it's never too late. Remember, the opera ain't over till the fat lady sings. Yogi Berra said, "It ain't over till it's over." You ain't finished till God says you're finished. Stay faithful to your calling, whatever it is, and God will make a way.

Have Thine own way, Lord!
Have Thine own way!
Thou art the potter,
I am the clay!

Mold me and make me
After Thy will,
While I am waiting,
Yielded and still.

Have Thine own way, Lord!
Have Thine own way!
Wounded and weary,
Help me, I pray!
Power, all power
Surely is Thine!
Touch me and heal me,
Savior divine.

—Adelaide A. Pollard

Chapter Five

There's No Virtue in Handling a Rubber Snake

To conquer without risk
is to triumph without glory.[1]
—*Pierre Corneille*

NOT LONG AGO MY WIFE, Susan, and I
were scheduled to travel to Israel for ten days as guest speakers and teachers at a school there. Only a couple of weeks before we were due to depart, the school's director, with whom we had coordinated the dates, realized that he had inadvertently scheduled us for a time when the students would be on break. Now we faced a dilemma. Should we go ahead as planned or should we reschedule? On the one hand, we had already spent $3000 on the airline tickets, and changing them would cost another $1000. On the other hand, if we went ahead, what would we do at a school with no students present—just sit around for ten days?

As Susan and I prayed about this, I heard the Lord say to me, "If I want you to go there and sit around for ten days, then that's as important as going over there and doing anything else you could do." We simply did not have a peace about postponing our trip so, even though we did not fully understand why, we followed the peace and decided to go ahead with our original dates.

One morning a short time later the Lord gave me a vision. In my mind's eye I saw a man holding a serpent. He was with one of those Christian sects that handle live snakes as a demonstration of their faith (there are still some of those in Kentucky!). As I watched this snake handler I heard God say, "There is no virtue in handling a rubber snake."

"What?" I asked, confused.

He repeated, "There is no virtue in handling a rubber snake. These people, as wrong as they are, would never try to prove their faith by handling a rubber snake. There has to be an element of risk in order for a test of faith to be a legitimate test."

Please understand that I neither believe in nor advocate snake handling as an element of faith. Such a practice is a way-out extreme that goes far beyond any biblical guidelines. However, as a test of faith, there *is* no virtue in handling a rubber snake because there is no chance for it to turn around and bite you. There is no risk involved in handling a rubber snake.

The point that God was making is that if we are going to serve and follow Him, there is a certain amount of risk that we must be willing to accept. There are times when we simply have to step out in faith, regardless of how things appear. Our decisions should be motivated by our sense of God's will, not by our assessment of how safe those decisions are. Walking in obedience to Christ means being ready to move beyond our safety net.

Don't Worry About Your Safety Net

THE 1952 FILM *THE GREATEST SHOW ON EARTH* depicts the lives of performers in the Ringling Brothers and Barnum and Bailey Circus. One of the story lines tells of the escalating rivalry between two trapeze artists, a woman named Holly and a man known as the Great Sebastian, who are vying for the coveted position of center ring. Each one constantly tries to outdo the other in the air even as romance blossoms between them on the ground. Their competition grows more and more intense until one day the Great Sebastian on impulse cuts down his safety net just before performing. Moments later during his act, he misses a jump and plummets to the ground. Alive but seriously injured, he insists of those who rush over to help him, "Walk me off. Don't deny me my exit."

Many people, including many Christians, behave as if the primary objective of life is to get by with minimal inconvenience and risk. Sometimes it seems as though everybody is looking for his or her "safety net." In a way this is understandable. After all, taking risks is scary. The Great Sebastian discovered firsthand how dangerous life can be when you operate without a safety net. What we sometimes forget is that the very act of living from day to day carries certain unavoidable risks. Life itself is risky.

One of the lessons of human history is that few significant achievements, accomplishments, or advancements have come about without someone somewhere taking a risk. Remember the old saying, "Nothing ventured, nothing gained." Herodotus, the ancient Greek historian, wrote, "Great deeds are usually wrought at great risks." General Douglas MacArthur said, "There is no security on this earth. Only opportunity." If we insist on security above all else, we will miss the opportunities to expand ourselves and become all we can be. Capitalizing on our opportunities requires the willingness to take risks.

There are many believers who want to serve the Lord, but only if they know their safety net is securely in place. They want a form of devotion to Christ but are not interested in the reality. Before they step out and try anything, they want to be sure that nothing will turn around and bite them. Their approach to the Christian life is like handling a rubber snake; it looks good on the surface but doesn't accomplish anything.

Whenever we serve the Lord, there is an element of risk. There is a risk that we will be misunderstood. There is a risk that we will be ridiculed. There is a risk that we will be persecuted. There is a risk that we will make mistakes and yes, there is a risk that we will *fail*.

A lot of people who talk about stepping out in faith aren't really willing to unless they have a safety net. That is not genuine faith. True faith is venturing out onto the trapeze of life without a safety net and trusting the Lord to catch us if (and when) we fall. Years ago there was a popular description of faith that read, "Faith is walking to the edge of all the light you have—and taking one more step."

Reasonable risk taking is a way of exercising our faith, as long as we are responding to the Lord's drawing in our hearts and not simply trying to put Him to a foolish test. We can discover greater richness and fullness to life when we "step out on a limb" from time to time because we discover for ourselves the Lord's ability and faithfulness to take care of us. In Matthew 14:25-31, when Peter walked on the water at Jesus' invitation, he had no safety net. All he had was his trust in Jesus. Even though Peter's faith faltered in that instance and

Jesus had to rescue him, Peter learned a lot more about the Lord (and about himself) than he ever would have if he had never gotten out of the boat.

There is no way that we can anticipate or prepare for every possible twist or turn that life can take. Even the most carefully prepared safety net can fail unexpectedly. That's why faith is so important. It's no accident that the Bible refers to the Christian life as a walk of faith. Paul said, "We live by faith, not by sight" (2 Cor. 5:7). The Lord is perfectly capable of taking care of us in any and every circumstance. He does not need us to busy ourselves all the time trying to orchestrate every element of our security and welfare. He wants us to trust Him.

Don't Compromise Your Principles for the Sake of Security

DON'T MISUNDERSTAND ME. I am not saying that there is no place for Christians giving careful and prayerful consideration to wise financial planning for their future and that of their families; there *is*. What I *am* saying is that we should never let our concern for security override our readiness to obey God's will. Sometimes the Lord will tell us to do something that makes no logical sense by human reason. We should never compromise our principles or our obedience for the sake of our personal security.

I am a member of a small outgrowing denomination that is a conservative, evangelical, and charismatic offshoot of a major mainstream American denomination. The parent denomination has taken some very liberal turns in recent years that have left many of its more conservative clergy and laity very uncomfortable. For example, the denomination recently consecrated its first African-American female bishop. There's nothing at all wrong with that as far as it goes, except that the decision was not made based on her merits as a woman of God. She was consecrated a bishop *because* she is a woman, *because* she is African-American, and *because* she is a practicing lesbian. It was their way of saying, "See how up-to-date with the times we are!" How much more politically correct could you get?

On occasion I have spoken with a number of the more conservative clergymen in this denomination who have expressed to me their discomfort and disapproval of the direction their denomination is going. I often ask, "Why do you stay there? Why don't you come join us? You're more than welcome, and you would be much more comfortable." A common reply I hear is, "What about my pension?"

Granted, some of them may have good and legitimate reasons for staying. They may even feel that perhaps they can be a positive and corrective influence. Others, however, may be allowing their concern for their security in the future to take precedence over their principles and obedience in the present.

Whenever we place too much faith in a man-made safety net, we tend to take our eyes and our trust away from the Lord. As a result, we end up focusing on the things and patterns of the world, which cause our spiritual priorities to become all screwed up.

God Is the Only Safety Net We Need

THE MIND-SET AND PHILOSOPHY of the world have infiltrated the Church to such a degree that we often think and act like the world without fully realizing it. We assume that we alone are responsible for "feathering our own nest" and making provision for both our present and our future needs. This sense of rugged self-reliance among American Christians is due in large measure to the so-called "Protestant work ethic" as well as to a culture of independence that prizes self-made success.

Both of these influences are intrinsic to American society, and both have biblical foundations. The Protestant work ethic values hard, honest labor in making a living and in bearing the responsibility for supporting one's family without being a burden on the state. These values are based on the fact that work was part of the original activity of man in the Garden of Eden prior to the fall. Work was part of God's original design. Further support comes from verses such as: "For even when we were with you, we gave you this rule: 'If a man will not work, he shall not eat' " (2 Thess. 3:10), and "If anyone does not provide for his relatives, and especially for his immediate family, he has denied the faith and is worse than an unbeliever" (1 Tim. 5:8). The concept of independence derives from the fact that man was created as a free being in relationship with God, and that the overall message of the Bible is how God brings freedom and redemption to all people through Christ.

While all of this is true, at the same time we must never forget that ultimately we are totally dependent on the Lord for everything. One of the things that Jesus taught us to pray is, "Give us this day our daily bread." God may give us the health and the means to earn our daily bread, but we are still dependent on Him to provide it. Proverbs 3:5-6 urges us to: "Trust in the Lord with all your heart and lean not on your own understanding; in all your ways acknowledge Him, and He will make your paths straight."

Jesus taught the same truth when He said:

*So do not worry, saying, "What shall we eat?" or
"What shall we drink?" or "What shall we wear?"
For the pagans run after all these things, and your
heavenly Father knows that you need them. But seek
first His kingdom and His righteousness, and all
these things will be given to you as well. Therefore
do not worry about tomorrow, for tomorrow will
worry about itself. Each day has enough trouble of
its own* (Matthew 6:31-34).

God is the only safety net we need. He is perfectly capable of taking care of every provision. His way of handling your needs may be very different from His way of handling mine. If God places an opportunity before you to make money through a business of your own, or through success in the stock market, or some such thing, don't shy away from it. Embrace it with a thankful heart and pursue it with diligence. The important thing is learning how to follow God's leading in your life and to recognize how He is working in your situation.

In the case of my present ministry, I believe the Lord has led me simply to trust Him and seek no other safety net. That is His plan for me, and I have had to learn to accept it. It has been a real faith-builder for me, and that may be one reason why He has taken me in this direction. On the surface, it often appears that financial insolvency is a snake ready to reach back and bite me at any moment. The reality, however, is that God is faithful to provide. I just have to keep walking in faith.

It's not always easy. One time years ago, back in the early days of rebuilding my ministry, we came down to the place where we didn't have a paycheck for nine months. I had a black powder gun collection that I was really proud of. I sold it. I also sold the collection of Civil War art that I had been building. I sold all my jewelry and Susan sold all of the household items we didn't need to have. Finally, there was nothing left to sell, and we were pretty much broke. There was nothing for us to do except trust the Lord. We would come to the beginning of a month and feel that there was no possible way to make it to the end of the month, and yet we made it through. Then, looking back, we could see the footprints of the Lord and how He had brought us through. We saw in hindsight what we could not perceive while we were going through it. Although we didn't understand exactly how God did it, we knew that He had taken care of us.

That was probably some of the most valuable time I've ever spent in the ministry, because God showed me that He is my source, and I can trust Him. During those nine months without a paycheck we never missed a payment, we never incurred a late charge, and we never missed a meal. We never missed anything, because God took care of us.

God is the only safety net we need.

It's Not a Job; It's a Calling

THE UNITED STATES NAVY HAS USED as a recruiting slogan, "It's not a job; it's an adventure." The same could be said about the Christian life. Whatever else we might say or think about our lives as believers, I think it is safe to say that being a Christian is certainly not boring! At least it shouldn't be. A life of faith that depends moment by moment on the guidance and provision of God always has an element of adventure.

Another way to look at our lives as Christians is to modify the slogan a bit and say, "It's not a job; it's a calling." As long as we keep clearly in mind the difference between the two, we're fine. It's when we confuse one with the other that we get into trouble. Seeing our ministry, whatever it may be, as a divine calling helps us keep everything in perspective and properly focus our spiritual priorities. Frequently, energy sappers such as relentless barrages of criticism or long months of labor with little visible results, can drain our enthusiasm and leave us discouraged and disillusioned. When we lose sight and sense of our call, we tend to start looking at our ministry as a "job." That's when we are in great danger of being swept up into professionalism.

There are two ways to define professionalism. On the one hand, it means maintaining and presenting a professional attitude toward what we do. We take pride in our work and seek to apply our greatest skill and ability to every endeavor. Any task or ministry worth doing is worth doing well. This is the positive side of professionalism.

The negative side is when we reach the point where we are simply "performing" in order to preserve the status quo or where advancement to the next level is the most important goal of all, and everything else—even ministering to people—takes second place. Negative professionalism sidetracks our attention from substance and places a greater emphasis on external trappings. In one sense it means "being in it for the money." The preachers who won't leave their liberal denomination for fear of losing their pensions have fallen into this trap. They have sacrificed the integrity and effectiveness of their ministries because they are too concerned about their external security. In their decision to maintain the status quo they have become "professional" ministers in the negative sense.

It's easy to get caught up in the wrong kind of "professional" attitude if you allow your view of success to be determined by your peers rather than by the Lord. How well I know! For years I did everything I could to make sure that I became and remained the top Christian comedian in the world. Sure, I was preaching the gospel. I cared about it and I loved the people who came to my concerts. Yet, I *had* to put out at least one album a year in order to be running with the "big boys." I *had* to be in *Contemporary Christian Music* magazine; I *had* to be on the charts. I *had* to do all of these things because that is what defined "success" in the crowd I was running with. There were certain things I simply had to do in order to sit down in the company of certain people and consider myself "one of the boys."

Once you get a taste of success, and particularly if you attain a national following, it is so easy to fall into the "show business" mentality. Back when I was performing before thousands in large halls, I tried to arrive about 15 minutes before I was supposed to go on. I had a road manager that had already been there for hours setting everything up. I would walk in the back door, my road manager would hand me a diet soda, and I would go in for about five minutes of prayer with whoever was there. Then I would ask my road manager how many people were in the house, he would tell me, and then I would go out there and do my thing. After the show I would come out, get my diet soda, head out the back door, and return to the hotel. I had all the trappings of stardom: private dressing room, my own airplane, fancy cars, a large and loyal following, and yada, yada, yada.

Part of my problem was that although I was surrounded by people who could make great business decisions, I did not have anyone who served as a spiritual advisor for me. There was no one who could say to me, "Mike, I was praying last night about this new idea you have, and God spoke to me. I have a real catch in my spirit about this. We need to take a closer look before we move in this direction." Or, "Mike, that new idea you had is great. I asked the Lord about it, and He has given me a real sense of peace. I think this is the direction we should go."

We were a professional "show biz" organization. There's not a single thing wrong with that as long as you make absolutely sure that that is what God wants you to do. In my case, my sense of ministry got lost in the swirl of professionalism. I was called to preach the gospel, p. s. I'm funny. However, the "p. s." became the body of the letter while the body—my calling to preach the gospel—became the postscript. Everything got all turned around, and when it was turned around it fell out of balance. It almost *had* to crash eventually.

One of the reasons I went through what I went through was so God could remind me of my calling and set me free from my career. He had to push me out of my "professional" mind-set so I could simply learn to be content as a man of God.

If You Rock the Boat, You May End up in the Water

SOMETIMES GOD HAS TO SHAKE some of us up to get our eyes off ourselves and back on Him where they belong. If we get stuck in the status quo when the Lord wants to move on, He will do whatever He needs to do to get us unstuck. If we "kick against the goads" and resist Him long enough, He will let us have our way and go on without us. If we end up sidelined in ministry as a result, it is our own fault.

On the other hand, we might be blindsided by those who think that we are threatening *their* status quo. Most people don't take kindly to someone else upsetting their gig. Sometimes the boat needs to be rocked, but as often as not, he who rocks the boat is the first one to end up in the water.

That's what caused Jesus to get into trouble with the scribes and Pharisees. Jesus was a boat-rocker. His enemies did not oppose Him, reject Him, and hate Him because they believed He was teaching heresy as much as because they considered Him a threat to their secure positions. They were the respected scholars and experts on the law and the paragons of virtue that everyone else should admire and imitate. At least, that's how they saw themselves. Then all of a sudden a lowly carpenter's son shows up and begins exposing the chinks in their armor—the sin and hypocrisy they have hidden beneath a thin veneer of piety. Many of these men were religious frauds and they hated Jesus for exposing them to the light. In the end, that's why they killed Him.

Many believers today have become victims of "friendly fire" because they were viewed as threats to the structure (*ekklesia*). Whether knowingly or not, they tried to rock the boat and got tossed overboard for their trouble. Most people fear and resist change, particularly those who are tradition-bound. Anyone who comes to them with a new idea or a fresh way of doing things or who suggests that God may be moving in a different direction is greeted with fear, suspicion, and often, anger.

If you have been tossed out of the boat—for whatever reason—and find yourself thrashing about in the waves, remember the example of Peter. As long as he looked only to Jesus as his safety net, he walked on the water. Jesus can do the same for you. If the crew of the *S.S. Ekklesia* has made you walk the plank, trust yourself to the mercy of the One who is the Master of the winds and the waves.

Don't be afraid of the challenge. Little in this life that is worthwhile is accomplished without risk. There is no virtue in handling a rubber snake. "Trust in the Lord with all your heart and lean not on your own understanding; in all your ways acknowledge Him, and He will make your paths straight" (Prov. 3:5-6).

Meditate on the words of this prayer, called the Breton Fisherman's Prayer:

> Protect me, oh Lord, for my boat is so small;
> Protect me, oh Lord, for my boat is so small.
> My boat is so small and your sea is so wide;
> Protect me, oh Lord.

ENDNOTE

1. Pierre Corneille, quoted in *Bartlett's Familiar Quotations, 16th ed.* by John Bartlett, Justin Kaplan, ed. (New York: Little, Brown and Co., 1992), 249:9.

Chapter Six

YOU'VE GOT TO BE BROKEN TO BE REBUILT

Strong at the Broken Places[1]
—Max Cleland

ONE OF THE HIT TELEVISION SHOWS of the late 1970s was a science fiction series called *The Six Million Dollar Man*. The premise: An astronaut named Steve Austin, severely injured in the crash of an experimental NASA aircraft, receives cybernetic replacements for his left eye, right arm, and both legs, making him the world's first "bionic" man. The voice-over narration at the beginning says, "We can rebuild him. We have the technology. We can make him better than he was before. Better, stronger, faster."

With all his bionic enhancements Steve Austin could run faster, jump higher, see farther, and perform greater feats of strength than ordinary humans. Sounds great, doesn't it? There was only one problem: Before Steve Austin could become bionic he had to suffer being all bashed up. He had to be broken before he could be rebuilt.

The same thing is true in life. Remember the old adage, "If it ain't broke, don't fix it"? There is a lot of truth in that. Only broken things need to be fixed. God's Word says that all of mankind has been "broken" by sin. The "fix" is forgiveness of sin made possible by the death of Christ. Before any of us can be "rebuilt," we have to recognize that we are broken. That is part of the ministry of the Holy Spirit in our lives. He makes us aware of our own sinfulness and awakens us to our need for repentance and forgiveness. When we turn to Christ in faith He comes in and "fixes" us.

Sometimes we need to be fixed even after we are saved. "Friendly fire" can break our spirit and shatter our confidence, leaving us just as crippled in soul as Steve Austin was in body. That is when we must look to the Lord to rebuild us.

I had been so broken by all that I had gone through that I began to manifest physical symptoms. I couldn't sleep. I was listless and short-tempered. The most telling sign, however, was the huge hives that would appear on my body. They were the size of saucers, were itchy, and were bright red. If anyone ever needed fixing, it was me. I would sit, scratch, and think of Job. Job's confession became my war cry: "Though He slay me, yet will I trust in Him" (Job 13:15 KJV). When you get to the place where all you have is Jesus, He turns out to be all you need.

God Prefers to Use Broken People

STEVE AUSTIN AND HIS BIONIC EN-HANCEMENTS are fiction. In the same way, there is no such thing as a "bionic" Christian. Christians are not extraordinary people with superhuman or supernatural abilities, but ordinary folks who know a superhuman and supernatural God. It is only when we recognize our weaknesses and our limitations that we get to the place where the Lord can use us effectively. The clear witness both of history and of the Word of God is that the people God uses most effectively are those who have been broken—who have cast themselves completely on God's mercy because they have nothing else—and have allowed Him to rebuild them.

King David of Israel was a man after God's own heart, but he also knew what it was to be broken and restored. He had firsthand knowledge of God's faithfulness in responding to the cries of the broken:

> *The Lord is close to those who are of a broken heart and saves such as are crushed with sorrow for sin and are humbly and thoroughly penitent* (Psalm 34:18, AMP).

> *My sacrifice [the sacrifice acceptable] to God is a broken spirit; a broken and a contrite heart [broken down with sorrow for sin and humbly and thoroughly penitent], such, O God, You will not despise* (Psalm 51:17, AMP).

Broken people are good material for rebuilding because they know how weak and flawed they are, and how prone they are to temptation, sin, and mistakes. This knowledge makes them more aware of how totally dependent they are on the Lord. God uses people who know they can do nothing without Him.

Consider Moses. Raised in Egypt as the adopted son of Pharaoh, Moses had everything going for him: education, wealth, authority, power. His first attempt to deliver his fellow Hebrews backfired, however, and he was forced to flee the country as an outcast and a fugitive wanted for murder. He spent the next 40 years tending sheep on the backside of the desert of Midian, until the day his encounter with the Lord at a burning bush on Mount Sinai brought the whole purpose of his life into sharp focus. Moses was broken...and became God's chosen deliverer of Israel.

What about Simon Peter? The brash and boastful fisherman, hotheaded and impulsive, was brought face-to-face with his own human weaknesses one night in the courtyard of the high priest's house. Mere hours after loudly proclaiming his unshakeable loyalty to Jesus, Peter denied three times that he even knew Him. When the chips were down Peter disclaimed Jesus because he feared for his own skin. Peter was humbled and devastated at seeing the darkness of his own character. Then came that morning on the lakeshore when the risen Christ gently asked three times, "Simon, do you love Me?" Simon Peter was broken...and became a pillar of the early Church, an apostle and fearless preacher of the gospel who fully lived up to the nickname Jesus gave him—"the Rock."

Don't forget Saul of Tarsus. Proud Pharisee, a self-acknowledged "Hebrew of the Hebrews," and persecutor of Christians, Saul was knocked off his high horse (literally!) on the road to Damascus by a vision of the risen Christ. Blinded and humbled, Saul spent three days in physical darkness in order that he could receive spiritual light. Saul was broken...and became Paul, the apostle to the Gentiles and the greatest evangelist and missionary in the history of the Church.

God prefers to use broken people. As a matter of fact, it is only broken people who can enjoy the intimate presence of the Lord—broken people who long for His healing touch. When it comes to mankind, God is always in the rebuilding and restoring business. This promise from Isaiah makes His intentions unmistakable:

> For this is what the high and lofty One says—He who lives forever, whose name is holy: "I live in a high and holy place, but also with him who is contrite and lowly in spirit, to revive the spirit of the

lowly and to revive the heart of the contrite. I will not accuse forever, nor will I always be angry, for then the spirit of man would grow faint before Me— the breath of man that I have created. I was enraged by his sinful greed; I punished him, and hid My face in anger, yet he kept on in his willful ways. I have seen his ways, but I will heal him; I will guide him and restore comfort to him, creating praise on the lips of the mourners in Israel. Peace, peace, to those far and near," says the Lord. "And I will heal them" (Isaiah 57:15-19).

Susan and I have been blessed to become friends with Roy and Mary Kendall, founders and directors of the School of Worship in Jerusalem. The school is a nine-month discipleship experience that we would highly recommend to anyone who longs to become a real worshiper of God.

As a result of our friendship with the Kendalls, we have become part of the school faculty as well. We travel to Israel once a year to teach and have fellowship with the students. We have come to know and love Jerusalem more than ever before.

My favorite church in the city is Saint Peter of the Crowing Rooster. This house of worship stands over the ancient home site of the high priest Caiaphas, the place where Peter denied knowing Jesus. The church is dedicated to all those who have ever failed and yet have been used by God any way. It is a wonderful place of peace and beauty. It makes you understand you are not the only one who Christ has had to "put back together again."

It's Not a Question of "Why?" but "What?"

IN THE PART OF KENTUCKY where I live, it is popular to use old brick as a construction material in building houses. There are two kinds of old brick: "reproduction" old brick, which is simply new brick made to look like old brick, and genuine old brick. Reproduction old brick is cheaper and easy to distinguish from genuine old brick (so what's the point?). Genuine old brick costs about four times as much because it requires the demolition of original, older structures and salvaging the brick from them. This is a more expensive process than manufacturing "new" old brick. In a way, it is a form of recycling: The old must be broken down in order to get the material for the new.

It is the same with old barn siding. A lot of folks like to use old barn wood for paneling in their homes. The only thing is, you have to knock down the barn if you want to use its wood to panel your walls.

When the Lord rebuilt my ministry, He used the material that was already there. Almost everything that I had built had to be knocked down so that He could take that "old brick" and build what *He* wanted to build. When God undertakes a rebuilding project, He takes the original material and uses it in completely new ways, in order to bring out new glory. When we give God our brokenness—our failures, our mistakes, our dashed hopes, our tattered dreams, and our chomped-on, chewed-up, and spit-out lives—He takes what we offer and builds a whole new beautiful structure according to His own design. We have to be willing to turn everything over to Jesus, holding nothing back:

I said, "Everything?"

He said, "Yes, everything."

I said, "Everything?"

He said, "Yes."

I said, "Some of it is perverse, sad, embarrassing."

He said, "Nevertheless..."

I said, "What will You do with it?"

He said, "If I can make an ax head float, turn water into wine, and cover this universe with one drop of My blood, I can take your mistakes and make them My victories!"

I said, "What about *my* victories?"

He said, "Those would only be more mistakes…"

Being broken and then rebuilt is never easy and always painful. In the midst of our pain, questions of every kind fill our minds. The biggest question of all is, "Why?"

When all of my trouble first started and it seemed as though I was being bombarded and attacked from every direction, I began questioning God. "Lord, why is this happening? Why are You letting them do this to me? Why won't You answer me? Why are You allowing me to go through this hell? Why me? Why, why, why?" The more I asked, "Why me?" the more I sensed the Lord saying, "Why not you? Who do you think you are that you should be spared what everybody else goes through?"

Slowly I began to understand what He meant. Whenever the Lord was blessing my life, I never stood before His throne asking, "Lord, why are You blessing me?" But just let something hard or painful come along and I started crying and complaining, "Oh, boo hoo, poor little me! Why is this happening?" It didn't matter that the trouble was there to challenge me or stretch me or cause me to grow. All I knew was that it hurt and I didn't like it. They may have been "growing pains," but they were keeping me awake at night.

I felt like I was being persecuted and that I was the only one who had ever suffered through anything like this. I thought my pain was so unique and so unfair. Before long, however, I learned that I was not alone. When I found out that other people—lots of people—had not only been through the same thing or something similar but also had survived, it was quite a revelation to me and encouraged me to stick it out.

One of the things I learned was not to ask why. That's the wrong question. There really is no answer to why. Instead, the Lord taught me to ask what. "What are You trying to say to me? What do You want me to do? What do You want me to learn from this? What will this experience teach me that will enable me to help somebody else?"

God never gives us anything that we cannot use to minister in the life of somebody else. He may give it to us initially to bring us where we need to be, but then He expects us to turn around and use what He has given us and what we have learned to help someone else.

It's Not Always the Devil's Fault

ESSENTIALLY, THE DIFFERENCE between why and what is a matter of perspective. The first is self-centered while the second is God-centered. Having a God-centered perspective goes a long way in helping us to endure the pain of adversity. Once we learn to view our experiences through the wider lens of the Lord's viewpoint, it is much easier to see how they fit into His greater overall purpose.

Something else that makes our trials easier to bear is understanding where they come from and how to properly respond to them. Every day we face challenges in life that come from any one of three sources: the devil, ourselves, or the Lord. How we respond to a particular trial or challenge depends on its source.

The most obvious source of our trials is satan. He is always ready to trip us up if we are not alert. How do we respond to the trials and temptations of the devil? James 4:7 gives us the key: "Submit yourselves, then, to God. Resist the devil, and he will flee from you." It is a two-step process. First, we must *submit* ourselves to God. Submission involves humility. Failure or refusal to submit to God is a sign of arrogance, stubbornness, and pride and will lead to certain defeat. None of us can go up against satan in our own strength; we will lose every time. Humbly submitting ourselves to God is recognition of our dependence on Him and connects us with His overcoming power.

After we submit to God, we are ready to *resist* the devil. God's Word promises that satan will flee from us when we resist him in the power of the Lord. One mistake many people make is giving up too easily. Some folks "resist" the devil for ten minutes and when he doesn't take off immediately they throw up their hands and quit trying. It may take ten minutes, ten days, or ten years. The key to victory is to resist and never give up. Stand firm in the power of the Holy Spirit and satan *will* flee from you.

Many of us in the Body of Christ have been taught that trials and challenges come only from the devil. Any trouble that pops up in our lives *must* be from him, right? I've got news for you. That's not necessarily true. It's not always the devil's fault. A second source of trouble is our own stupid mistakes or foolish choices. Sometimes we are our own worst enemy. Don't forget Pogo's comment, "We have met the enemy and he is us."

What do we do when *we* are the problem? Obviously, we can't cast ourselves out of ourselves, nor can we flee from ourselves. The best way to respond in this case is to *learn* from our mistakes. It may mean eating a heaping helping of humble pie, but that's a small price to pay for wisdom and maturity. We need to confess our mistakes or sins to God, claim His forgiveness, and move on, trusting Him for the strength and wisdom not to make the same mistake again.

In the third case, trials and challenges come our way as discipline from the Lord. That is an unfamiliar and uncomfortable concept for some believers, but true nonetheless. Discipline is an evidence of sonship and daughtership; an indication that God loves us and regards us as His own children: "My son, do not despise the Lord's discipline and do not resent His rebuke, because the Lord disciplines those He loves, as a father the son he delights in" (Prov. 3:11-12).

How should we respond to the Lord's discipline? God loves us and has our very best interests at heart. Anything He sends our way is for our good and ultimate benefit. We should teach ourselves to *embrace* those trials and challenges that come from the Lord because they are designed to build character in us. Character is a distinguishing mark of any mature Christian as well as any mature ministry. Just as we strengthen our physical muscles through the pain and exertion of exercise, so we strengthen our character through the pain of testing. The only way to develop character is in the crucible of trials, hardship, pain, and suffering. Remember, "No pain, no gain," and "No guts, no glory" are true both in our physical and our spiritual lives.

God uses adversity in our lives to refine our character and to guide us in the way of holiness, righteousness, and peace. Isaiah 48:10-11a says, "See, I have refined you, though not as silver; I have tested you in the furnace of affliction. For My own sake, for My own sake, I do this." The writer of the Book of Hebrews puts the whole thing in perspective:

Endure hardship as discipline; God is treating you as sons. For what son is not disciplined by his father? If you are not disciplined (and everyone undergoes discipline), then you are illegitimate children and not true sons. Moreover, we have all had human fathers who disciplined us and we respected them for it. How much more should we submit to the Father of our spirits and live! Our fathers disciplined us for a little while as they thought best; but God disciplines us for our good, that we may share in His holiness. No discipline seems pleasant at the time, but painful. Later on, however, it produces a harvest of righteousness and peace for those who have been trained by it (Hebrews 12:7-11).

Adversity is a part of life, and how we respond will either make us or break us. When it comes from the devil, we should *submit* ourselves to God and *resist* satan in the Spirit's power. If our problems come because we screwed up, the solution is to *humbly confess* to the Lord, seek to *learn* from our mistakes, and ask for the strength to avoid making them again. Whenever we find ourselves under the Lord's discipline, we should *embrace* it and ask Him to show us what He wants us to learn from it.

How Do You Know the Difference?

IT'S ONE THING TO UNDERSTAND that adversity can come from three different sources; it is another thing entirely to discern the specific source of any particular trial. How do you tell the difference?

For one thing, keep in mind that satan seeks our destruction while God seeks our salvation. Whenever God tests us, no matter how painful or difficult it may seem, His purpose is to refine, purify, strengthen, and mature us. The devil seeks only to destroy us. If you find yourself in a situation that is leading you down the path to destruction, you can be guaranteed that the devil is behind it, particularly if the spot you are in is through no fault of your own or due to circumstances beyond your control. Ask the Lord for discernment.

On the other hand, if you are in a bind because you messed up, you will know it deep down inside if you are honest with yourself. You will sense that something is not quite right, or maybe even hear a little voice inside warning, "You're screwing up! Watch out!" Every time we exercise our own will, we wind up getting exactly what we deserve, which isn't much. If the tough spot you are in is your own fault, the best thing to do is come clean about it. Just stand up and admit, "I was wrong." Get out of yourself and back into God's plan for your life. There comes a time when you simply have to own up to your own faults. That's what I had to do as part of my restoration, and it was one of the hardest things I've ever done in my life.

Trials that come as part of the Lord's testing and discipline, no matter how hard and painful they may feel, will be tempered by an undercurrent of abiding peace, a peace that defies human explanation because it is not of human origin. God's peace can sustain us in the storms of life and carry us safely to the other side. In Philippians Paul calls it the "peace...which transcends all understanding" (Phil. 4:7). The Amplified Bible really captures the full flavor of Paul's thought:

> *Do not fret or have any anxiety about anything, but in every circumstance and in everything, by prayer and petition (definite requests), with thanksgiving, continue to make your wants known to God. And God's peace [shall be yours, that tranquil state of a soul assured of its salvation through Christ, and so fearing nothing from God and being content with its earthly lot of whatever sort that is, that peace] which transcends all understanding shall garrison and mount guard over your hearts and minds in Christ Jesus* (Philippians 4:6-7, AMP).

Tribulation from the devil arouses fear and uncertainty; the Lord's testing, although often painful, also brings peace and the confident assurance that we will prevail because He is greater than the trials we face.

God Wants to Display His Work in Our Lives

THERE IS ANOTHER REASON why the Lord tests us and allows adversity into our lives: to display His presence, power, and work in us so that other people can see Him through us and come to know Him. This is a perspective on suffering that is beyond the world's comprehension. One day Jesus took advantage of the opportunity to teach this lesson to His disciples.

> *As He went along, He saw a man blind from birth. His disciples asked Him, "Rabbi, who sinned, this man or his parents, that he was born blind?" "Neither this man nor his parents sinned," said Jesus, "but this happened so that the work of God might be displayed in his life. As long as it is day, we must do the work of Him who sent Me. Night is coming, when no one can work. While I am in the world, I am the light of the world." Having said this, He spit on the ground, made some mud with the saliva, and put it on the man's eyes. "Go," He told him, "wash in the Pool of Siloam" (this word means Sent). So the man went and washed, and came home seeing* (John 9:1-7).

The blind man was blind through no fault of his own. His blindness was not because he screwed up or because his parents sinned. He was blind because he was born that way. Jesus used the man's adversity—his blindness—as an opportunity to reveal the power, goodness, and mercy of God. Because of his healing, the formerly blind man came to a saving knowledge of Christ and the righteous work of God was displayed in his life for others to see.

Why do we go through some of the things that we go through? So the work of God can be displayed in our lives. People sometimes ask me, "Brother Mike, you went through all that terrible stuff, the drugs, the alcohol, the occult, before you became a Christian. If Jesus loved you so much, why didn't He spare you from all that and save you while you were a child?" The only thing I can answer is, "Because the work of God needed to be displayed in my life."

As a Christian you may be going through tough times and wonder why. (Like I said before, "Why?" is the wrong question, but it is a perfectly natural one.) Perhaps you have experienced terrible family losses or disastrous financial reverses. Maybe you are sick and discouraged because you have prayed for healing that has not come. No matter what your situation, if you are a believer, God wants to display His work in your life.

Other people who know you are a Christian are watching you to see how you handle your adversity. If they see the peace of God in your life, and your patient, trusting endurance, they will see that God is real. They may realize that they can have God's peace in their lives and can trust Him to save them. Your hard road can become somebody else's pathway to eternal life.

Unbroken vessels tend to hide the light inside. Only when they are broken can they let their light shine. In the Book of Judges, when God used Gideon and three hundred men to deliver Israel from the Midianites, He instructed them to hide burning torches inside clay jars. At the right moment, all the men shattered the jars at the same time and shouted, "A sword for the Lord and for Gideon!" (Judg. 7:20b) God routed the Midianites and gave Gideon and his men complete victory.

God likes to use broken people because they know they are nothing and can do nothing without Him and have learned not to stand in His way or hide His light. Broken people eagerly yet humbly desire the Lord to fill them and use them because they have discovered that that is where true blessing and prosperity lie. Like Steve Austin, broken people who surrender themselves to the Lord for rebuilding are stronger and better for the experience. It is a physiological fact that broken bones when healed are strongest at the site of the break. Rebuilt believers can be used powerfully by God because they have become "strong at the broken places."

Let your brokenness become an altar upon which God can rebuild a life perfectly fitted and suited to His purpose. Reflect on the words of George Herbert:

> A broken ALTAR, Lord, thy servant rears,
> Made of a heart and cemented with tears;
> Whose parts are as thy hand did frame;
> No workman's tool hath touch'd the same.
> A HEART alone
> Is such a stone,
> As nothing but
> Thy pow'r doth cut.
> Wherefore each part
> Of my hard heart
> Meets in this frame
> To praise thy name.
> That if I chance to hold my peace,
> These stones to praise thee may not cease.
> Oh, let thy blessed SACRIFICE be mine,
> And sanctify this ALTAR to be thine.

ENDNOTE

1. *Strong at the Broken Places* is the title of Max Cleland's memoirs, originally published in 1980 and revised and republished in 2000 by Longstreet Press, Marietta, GA. Now a United States senator from Georgia, Max Cleland lost both

legs and one arm in a grenade blast in Vietnam. His book tells
the story of his struggle to recover from both the physical and
psychological effects of his wounds and how he learned to
become "strong at the broken places."

Chapter Seven

DON'T LET THE WORLD DEFINE WHO YOU ARE

You cannot become a great Christian…while
you yield yourself to the worldly maxims
and modes of business of men of the world.
—*Charles H. Spurgeon*

IN HIS 1982 FILM *ZELIG*, Woody Allen portrays Leonard Zelig, an emotionally insecure man whose hunger to fit in creates a psychological condition in which he literally becomes whoever he is with at the moment. If he is with a group of doctors, he becomes a doctor; when surrounded by overweight people he suddenly becomes heavy as well. Leonard Zelig is a human chameleon. With no clear identity of his own, he is shaped by the world around him.

Just as the standard garden-variety chameleon changes color to blend in with its background, Leonard Zelig develops an unusual condition in order to cope with his world. Because he lacks the strength of personality and character to shape his environment, he simply conforms to it. He finds security and safety in being just like everybody else.

To one degree or another almost all of us are like Leonard Zelig. Although we publicly applaud standout personalities for their "rugged individualism," privately we envy their courage while being perfectly happy ourselves just to remain "part of the crowd." Very few of us feel comfortable being singled out in a group, particularly if it draws embarrassing or unfavorable attention to us.

Some good friends of mine tried to dissuade me from writing this book. They warned me that the moment I do anything that brings attention to the ministry or myself, my critics will make another move. My friends are afraid that I will get hurt again. I appreciate their concern, but I can't let fear of what people might think or do keep me from accomplishing that which the Father has asked of me. I believe that people have to do their best and take their "licks." Anything else would be cowardice.

Conformity is easier and less painful than blazing a new trail. Just ask anyone who has ever run afoul of accepted social mores or religious traditions, or who has dared to step out in a different direction from the norm! Those who "march to a different drummer" are likely to have their legs shot out from under them for their trouble. Modern-day pharisees are always in the wings ready to pounce on anyone who has the gall to challenge the established order.

I'm not trying to foment meaningless rebellion here. After all, there is no point in rocking the boat just to rock the boat. Every now and then, however, the time comes to break out of the mold, to shake off the cobwebs of empty tradition and branch out in a new direction with revitalized enthusiasm and a fresh sense of purpose.

DON'T LET THE WORLD DEFINE WHO YOU ARE

Within the Body of Christ, *ekklesia* at its worst is the bastion of conformity. It discourages creative or "out-of-the-box" thinking, resists change, and pressures believers to unquestioningly toe a doctrinal or denominational line. Those who cross the line pay the consequences. Even when an individual genuinely screws up or makes an honest mistake, the punishment inflicted by the rest often far outweighs the magnitude of the offense. When it comes to the human weaknesses of our brothers and sisters in the faith, we Christians can sometimes be a very unforgiving lot.

"Friendly fire" can leave believers thoroughly disheartened and without the spirit or the will to continue. Even worse, they may start buying into the "bad press" that calls them worthless and unworthy. When life has you against the ropes reeling from a sucker punch, it's very easy to forget who you are and simply accept the world's assessment. Don't fall for that. Don't let the world define who you are; that's a false judgment anyway. Let the Word of God and the Spirit of Christ define you.

It Is in Christ That We Come to Know Our True Selves

AN ENVIRONMENT WHERE CONFORMITY is expected allows very little leeway for individual expression. Sometimes this is necessary. A good example is a military unit preparing for battle. Soldiers are trained to work together as a team to carry out the missions assigned to them by their superiors. Under these circumstances a freewheeling "do-your-own-thing" approach would have disastrous consequences. At the same time, however, soldiers who exhibit individual initiative within the parameters of the mission often make a

113

decisive difference in ensuring victory. That's the stuff of which heroes are made.

It is sad but true that many believers within the Body of Christ have traded their spiritual freedom and unique identity in Christ for legalistic conformity to man-made standards. True freedom scares some people because they don't know what to do with it. Life seems so much simpler when we know what to expect as well as what is expected of us.

The truest expression of the Christian life is freedom. Christ came to set us free from the bondage and blindness of sin into the liberty of eternal life in relationship with God. Jesus said, "If you hold to My teaching, you are really My disciples. Then you will know the truth, and the truth will set you free....I tell you the truth, everyone who sins is a slave to sin. Now a slave has no permanent place in the family, but a son belongs to it forever. So if the Son sets you free, you will be free indeed" (Jn. 8:31b-32; 34b-36). Thinking along the same lines, Paul wrote, "Therefore, there is now no condemnation for those who are in Christ Jesus, because through Christ Jesus the law of the Spirit of life set me free from the law of sin and death" (Rom. 8:1-2), and "It is for freedom that Christ has set us free. Stand firm, then, and do not let yourselves be burdened again by a yoke of slavery" (Gal. 5:1).

Christ has set us free to be ourselves, to celebrate our individuality and pursue our fullest potential. However, being a free individual is not the same as being independent. There is a big difference. As Christians we are not independent, but *dependent*—first on Christ, and then on each other. It is through our dependence upon Christ that we come to know our true selves. In Christ our true individuality is set free. We are also dependent upon one another as brothers and sisters in the Lord. There is no such thing as a "Lone Ranger" Christian. We need each other for mutual growth, maturity, encouragement, and accountability. That's why Jesus established His Church both as an assembly (*ekklesia* in its truest and best sense) and as a *fellowship* (*koinonia*) or *community* of believers; a *body* that functions properly only when all of its individual members work together in harmony and unity

Don't Conform to the World's Standards

IN JOHN 10:10, JESUS SAYS that He came to give us abundant life—life that overflows. Such abundance is possible only in a context of spiritual freedom. One of the greatest dangers to our experiencing the abundant life is discouragement. Whether we are beaten down by the criticism and low esteem of the world or by the shots fired at us by other believers, the effects can be crippling. When you feel like you have fallen as low as you can go it hardly seems worth the effort needed to get back up. Sometimes, in the midst of discouragement and despair, it seems much easier to sacrifice our hopes and dreams rather than fight for them, because they appear to be impossibly out of reach.

Discouragement is a mind-set of death. It is a documented fact that people with serious illnesses who become discouraged and lose hope are far less likely to recover than those who maintain an optimistic outlook. The general outlook of the world as a whole is the mind-set of death. This is no surprise, because the world as a whole is bound in sin, spiritual darkness, and death.

Jesus has called us to life, not death. He wants us to live, not die. Why then do we spend so much of our time listening to the negative, life-draining opinions and attitudes of the world? Why do we let the world continually beat us over the head and say, "You're worthless! Look how you screwed up!

You'll never amount to anything anymore. Once, you had everything going for you, but you blew it, big-time! Now you've lost it all! That's it, you're finished!"

All the while God is trying to get our attention. "Not so fast! What do they know? Listen to Me! I created you, so I know what you're made of." This is the God who said, "For I know the plans I have for you…plans to prosper you and not to harm you, plans to give you hope and a future" (Jer. 29:11). The world's assessment and your own personal setbacks notwithstanding, God has not rescinded that promise.

Don't conform to the world's standards, which lead to death, but to God's standards, which lead to abundant life. In his classic devotional book *My Utmost for His Highest*, Oswald Chambers wrote, "It is easier to sacrifice yourself than to fulfill your spiritual destiny."[1] The world expects you to offer yourself up on the dead altar of your failures. The Lord calls you to rise up and move forward into the fullness of His plan for you, which is more marvelous than you can imagine. As Oswald Chambers writes, "Beware of paying attention or going back to what you once were, when God wants you to be something that you have never been."[2]

The path to restoration and the fullness of God's abundant life lies not over the dead altar of failure but over the living altar of surrender and submission. I think Paul had this in mind when he wrote to the Romans:

> *Therefore, I urge you, brothers, in view of God's mercy, to offer your bodies as living sacrifices, holy and pleasing to God—this is your spiritual act of worship. Do not conform any longer to the pattern of this world, but be transformed by the renewing of your mind. Then you will be able to test and approve what God's will is—His good, pleasing and perfect will* (Romans 12:1-2).

Paul says that we are to do three things: offer our bodies as living sacrifices to God, refuse to conform to the pattern of the world, and be transformed by renewing our minds. How do we do this?

I was ministering once in Atascadero, California, where a state mental facility was located and hence the site of my sermon. At one point, one of the patients looked me in the face and, calmly announced, "You're crazy and they're never going to let you out of here." I thought to myself, *This guy has a lot of discernment and I'm glad I don't have my name stenciled on my underwear.* It was a funny incident, but what the patient had said was true. Unless our minds are dealt with, we will never know freedom.

Renewing our minds means, among other things, learning a new way of thinking; learning to think the way God thinks. This requires that we let go of the attitudes and thought patterns of the world. Being a living sacrifice means surrendering up everything in our lives that is not of God in order to experience abundant life, life in its fullest that those who are still of the world will never know.

How Do You Measure Success?

ONE OF THE THINGS WE HAVE TO GIVE UP is our tendency to measure success by the world's standards. A major problem among Christians today is that so many of us have bought into the world's concept of success. We may give good lip service to biblical principles of success, but in practice we have traded the wisdom of God's Word for the world's false idea that measures success by fame and fortune.

Although cultures differ widely around the world, one thing that almost all have in common is the view that success means having power, influence, and possessions. Americans tend to measure success in terms of owning a fancy car, living in a beautiful house, securing a high-paying job, being able to "keep up with the Joneses," having a perfect body, perfect teeth, perfect kids, etc. There are some societies in the world where a man who owns two goats is considered rich. Even in that case, however, his success and status hinge on the amount of his possessions.

This same materialistic view of success has seeped into the Body of Christ to the degree that it influences the way we think and virtually everything we do. The Church in America has become infatuated with the concept of "manyness" and "muchness." It has become our whole criterion for measuring success.

Sure, we hear people all the time saying, "Numbers don't count," but who are we kidding? Of course they do. After all, think of how many pastors are forced to resign their pulpits every year because their churches are not "growing" (translate: because they did not bring in a lot of new members and money). Who are the ones who get invited to preach or teach at all the major conferences? The folks with big churches or large, nationally known ministries.

Certainly, many of the "big guys" are where they are because they live in holy and humble surrender to the Lord and conduct their ministries with absolute integrity. God has blessed them because of this and also because they have been faithful to follow the calling He has given them. In our obsession with "manyness" and muchness," we tend to forget that true success is not a matter of size and numbers but of faithfulness to God's call.

The common idea today is that if you want to play with the "big boys" you have to have a big church or a major national ministry. Unspoken is the assumption that if you are "small potatoes" you obviously can't have anything important or significant to say.

What if the Lord has not called you to build a "big" church? What if His plan for you means living and working in a small and modest situation where hardly anyone outside your community or county will ever even know your name? If you buy into the lie that your worth is measured in large numbers and widespread recognition, you will spend your life beating yourself to death for nothing, simply because you failed to live up to a false standard of success.

God is not impressed with our "manyness" and "much-ness." He is only interested in seeing how obedient we are ready to be. True success means fulfilling our destiny, what-ever that destiny may be. It means finding God's will and pur-pose for our lives and carrying them out. True success is being faithful to God's call, be it big or small.

We need to stop thinking of success in the world's terms and start thinking of it in terms of fulfilling the destiny that God has established for us. How do we find that out? By stay-ing in communication with God. As we fellowship with the Lord through prayer and through His Word, He will begin to reveal to us our destiny in His purpose.

Sometimes when we lose sight of our destiny, God must take action to get us back on track. I spent 20 years as Ameri-ca's number-one Christian comedian, which would have been fine except that wasn't what God called me to be. He called me to be a minister of the gospel, p.s. I'm funny. It is always a big mistake to let your tools become who you are. Humor was my tool, my means to the end of preaching the gospel, but I allowed it to become an end in itself. I became career orient-ed instead of calling motivated.

This whole exercise of getting my butt whipped was God's way of setting me free from the bondage of my career and releasing me back into the freedom of my calling. I got knocked down but the Lord picked me up, dusted me off and put me back on the right road to my destiny. My calling is to preach the gospel to people who need to hear it, and as long as I am doing that, I am successful. It doesn't matter if I am preaching to five people, or five hundred, or five thousand; as long as I am preaching the gospel I am successful because I am doing what God has called me to do. I am fulfilling my destiny.

It took me a long time to understand that, but now that I do, I am truly content with where I am and what I am doing. I think I have come to know a little of how Paul felt when he wrote, "I have learned to be content whatever the circumstances. I know what it is to be in need, and I know what it is to have plenty. I have learned the secret of being content in any and every situation, whether well fed or hungry, whether living in plenty or in want. I can do everything through Him who gives me strength" (Phil. 4:11b-13).

The measure of our success is how well we fulfill our destiny. Success has nothing to do with material trappings like money, or externals such as fame or power. All of that is just "stuff." Stuff comes and goes; only what we do for the Kingdom of God lasts forever.

Blessed Are the Merciful

HOW WE MEASURE SUCCESS is one factor in determining whether we define ourselves or allow the world to define us; how we respond to attack is another. If we rise up and lash out every time somebody presses one of our "hot buttons," we are merely reacting to that person's behavior and allowing him or her to control us. Because we are sinners, the desire to retaliate when attacked is a "natural" response. If someone does us wrong we want vengeance or, at least, justice. Once we become Christians, the Lord calls us to a higher plane: mercy instead of vengeance and grace rather than justice.

At heart I am really a mercy and grace man, partly because God extended His mercy and grace to me and I know firsthand how wonderful they are. That's one of the reasons why I never pray for justice. Justice means getting what we deserve. As sinners we deserve hell. Mercy means being spared what we deserve, while grace gives us the opposite of what we deserve. I am very glad we have a just God, because that means we are all on an equal footing.

It's only natural for us to feel thankful and blessed when God extends His mercy and grace. But here is the real test: How do we feel when God extends that same mercy and grace to people we don't like—to people who have wounded us?

I had to wrestle with that question. How did I feel about God showing mercy and grace to all the people who attacked me? Would I feel better having enemies to hate and hold in contempt, while dreaming in my heart of the day when God's vengeance would fall on them? Or did I need to sit down and realize that they were His children too and that His mercy and grace were just as available and sufficient for their needs as they were for mine? If I took the view that God's mercy and grace extended to them too, how would that affect my relationship with them?

Jesus had a lot to say on the subject. A large portion of the Sermon on the Mount in Matthew 5–7 is devoted to teaching us how we should relate to and treat other people. Listen to how Jesus describes children of God; some of it sounds like a catalog of broken people: "Blessed are the poor in spirit...blessed are those who mourn...blessed are the meek... blessed are those who hunger and thirst for righteousness..." (Mt. 5:3-6). Then He continues, "Blessed are the merciful... blessed are the pure in heart...blessed are the peacemakers...blessed are those who are persecuted because of righteousness..." (Mt. 5:7-10). Jesus is still talking about the same folks!

No matter how badly we may have been hurt by someone else, if we take the gospel of Jesus Christ seriously, there is no room in our lives for hatred, bitterness, or the thirst for vengeance:

> *Therefore, if you are offering your gift at the altar and there remember that your brother has something against you, leave your gift there in front of the altar. First go and be reconciled to your brother; then come and offer your gift"* (Matthew 5:23-24).

> *You have heard that it was said, "Eye for eye, and tooth for tooth." But I tell you, Do not resist an evil person. If someone strikes you on the right cheek, turn to him the other also. And if someone wants to sue you and take your tunic, let him have your cloak as well. If someone forces you to go one mile, go with him two miles. Give to the one who asks you, and do not turn away from the one who wants to borrow from you. You have heard that it was said, "Love your neighbor and hate your enemy." But I tell you: Love your enemies and pray for those who persecute you....Be perfect, therefore, as your heavenly Father is perfect* (Matthew 5:38-44,48).

By the grace of God, today I do not have a root of bitterness festering in my heart that would prevent me from experiencing His love myself. I had to learn that if I was not willing for God to be merciful to everybody else, then I could not expect Him to be merciful to me. If His mercy doesn't extend to everyone—even to those who hurt me the most—then it doesn't extend to me.

God's mercy, grace, and forgiveness are available to *anyone* who repents. He loves everyone unconditionally. How comfortable are we with that? We have to be comfortable with it; otherwise we have no right to be comfortable with the fact that God loves *us*. Mercy and grace are costly; they cost God the life of His Son. They will cost us our pride.

It All Comes Down to Pride

PRIDE IS THE ROOT OF ALL SIN. Ultimately, every sinful thought, word, or deed has its source in pride. What was the reason for satan's fall? Pride. He said, "I want to be like God," then tried to fulfill his desire. Satan did not say he wanted to *be* God; he was smart enough to know that there was only one show in town. He presumed to be *like* God, and his pride was his downfall. It was the same with Adam and Eve. They took satan's bait—the pride of thinking they could become like God—with disastrous results.

No matter who we are, we struggle with pride every day. If, through the power of the Holy Spirit, we can learn to deal with our pride, we can learn to deal with everything else, because pride is at the core. The idea that God's mercy and grace extend to our enemies is a real blow to our pride, because pride says, "They owe me, big-time; after what they did to me, they deserve whatever payback they get." When we learn to crucify our pride and put it to death on the cross with Christ, we will no longer care about payback. If the root is destroyed, the tree cannot grow.

Before we can come to the place where we can really crucify our pride, we have to be able to understand the depth of God's mercy. That's why I believe a lot of us miss the point when we say something like, "That's all right, I won't worry about getting even. Vengeance belongs to God. He will take care of it." What we are really saying is that we still want vengeance meted out to our enemies, but we are willing to let God be the "heavy." We want to see Him come down like some supernatural "enforcer" and slap people around, knock a few heads together or break a few arms.

That's not the way God is. If we want to know what God is like, all we have to do is look at Jesus. He said that we should turn the other cheek, walk the second mile, love our enemies, and pray for those who persecute us. The only way we can do any of these is by killing our pride.

Our response to ill treatment should be the opposite of how the world would respond. On this point the apostle Paul provides wise, godly counsel:

Bless those who persecute you; bless and do not curse. Rejoice with those who rejoice; mourn with those who mourn. Live in harmony with one another. Do not be proud, but be willing to associate with people of low position. Do not be conceited. Do not repay anyone evil for evil. Be careful to do what is right in the eyes of everybody. If it is possible, as far as it depends on you, live at peace with everyone. Do not take revenge, my friends, but leave room for God's wrath, for it is written: "It is mine to avenge; I will repay," says the Lord. On the contrary: "If your enemy is hungry, feed him; if he is thirsty, give him something to drink. In doing this, you will heap burning coals on his head." Do not be overcome by evil, but overcome evil with good (Romans 12:14-21).

Vengeance belongs to the Lord, and He will repay. This is not a salve to soothe our bruised pride. What this means is that God is the *only* one who has the authority to mete out vengeance; we do not. Because God is just, we can trust Him to do all things well. The next time you're tempted to ask God to take vengeance on your enemy, think about this: *What if God decided to answer your enemy's prayer to take vengeance on you?* Remember that Jesus said, "Do to others as you would have them do to you" (Lk. 6:31).

When we can put aside our desire for vengeance, God is free to work in our hearts and lives to vindicate us before men. Whether we have been slandered or attacked unfairly, or whether we suffer the consequences of our own mistakes, the Lord can restore us and vindicate us if we will leave it in His hands. Vindication is the work that the Lord wants to do in us, and that is where our focus should be. We should not worry about what happens to our enemies or to those who have hurt us. They are in God's hands and He will take care of them in His own time and in His own way. Instead, we should pray that they receive the same mercy and grace from the Lord that we have received.

It is so easy for us to fall into the attitudes and thought processes of the world that we have to be on our guard all the time. Our destiny is not to be like Leonard Zelig, shaped by his world and changing like the wind to conform to whatever environment he is in. God has called us instead to be shapers of the world, to engage our contemporary culture and society with the truth of the unchanging gospel of Jesus Christ, which has the power to transform the world.

Don't let the world define who you are. God has already defined you—you are His beloved child, redeemed through the blood of Jesus. Don't allow the mistakes of your past or the hardships of your present to hold you back. Step forward with confidence into the destiny the Lord has for you—a destiny to help change the world one person at a time. Reflect on this beautiful prayer, attributed to Francis of Assisi:

> Lord, make me an instrument of Your peace;
> Where there is hatred, let me sow love;
> Where there is injury, pardon;
> Where there is doubt, faith;
> Where there is despair, hope;
> Where there is darkness, light;
> Where there is sadness, joy.
> O Divine Master, grant that I may not so much seek
> To be consoled as to console;
> To be understood as to understand;
> To be loved as to love;
> For it is in giving that we receive,
> It is in pardoning that we are pardoned,
> It is in dying that we are born to eternal life.

ENDNOTES

1. Oswald Chambers, *My Utmost For His Highest*, devotional for June 8, Copyright © 1992 by Oswald Chambers Publications Association, Ltd. Original edition copyright © 1935 by Dodd, Mead & Company, Inc. Copyright renewed 1963 by Oswald Chambers Publications Association, Ltd. All Rights reserved. United States publication rights are held by Discovery House Publishers, which is affiliated with RBC Ministries, Grand Rapids, Michigan 49512. Electronic Edition STEP Files Copyright © 1998, Parsons Technology, Inc., all rights reserved.

2. Oswald Chambers, *My Utmost For His Highest*, devotional for June 8.

Chapter Eight

It's Time to Launch Out Into the Deep

To be, rather than to seem to be,
a friend of God.
—*Gregory of Nazianzus*

As LONG AS WE ARE CONTENT to simply stand on the shore and watch the waves roll in, we will never experience the depths of abundant life in the Spirit. Remember that nothing truly worthwhile is accomplished without risk. If we want to fulfill our destiny, we must be willing to launch out into the deep, even if all we have to go on is the Word of the Lord. His Word is sufficient for any situation.

What if Peter, Andrew, James, and John had not listened to Jesus when He called them? They would have continued in their trade as successful professional fishermen, but would have missed their higher destiny as apostles. They might never have known the joys of intimate fellowship with the Lord.

One day as Jesus was standing by the Lake of Gennesaret, with the people crowding around Him and listening to the word of God, He saw at the water's edge two boats, left there by the fishermen, who were washing their nets. He got into one of the boats, the one belonging to Simon, and asked him to put out a little from shore. Then He sat down and taught the people from the boat. When He had finished speaking, He said to Simon, "Put out into deep water, and let down the nets for a catch." Simon answered, "Master, we've worked hard all night and haven't caught anything. But because You say so, I will let down the nets." When they had done so, they caught such a large number of fish that their nets began to break. So they signaled their partners in the other boat to come and help them, and they came and filled both boats so full that they began to sink. When Simon Peter saw this, he fell at Jesus' knees and said, "Go away from me, Lord; I am a sinful man!" For he and all his companions were astonished at the catch of fish they had taken, and so were James and John, the sons of Zebedee, Simon's partners. Then Jesus said to Simon, "Don't be afraid; from now on you will catch men." So they pulled their boats up on shore, left everything and followed Him (Luke 5:1-11).

Jesus said to Simon, "Put out into deep water, and let the nets down for a catch." What audacity, this "landlubber" trying to tell an experienced fisherman how to fish! Simon and the others had just pulled an all-nighter at the nets, with nothing to show for their efforts. The fish simply could not be found. Had any other man made the request, hotheaded Simon might have blown his stack. There was something different, though, about Jesus. Simon simply replied, "Master...because You say so, I will let down the nets."

Obeying the words of Jesus led these tough, sturdy fishermen to an experience and a revelation that transformed their lives. Suddenly their nets were full of fish in what may have been the largest catch of their careers. At the same time, their eyes were opened to new possibilities: a greater destiny than they had ever dreamed, and an intimacy with God that they would never have thought possible.

Abundant Life Means Intimacy With God

THE MIRACULOUS CATCH OF FISH revealed Jesus in a divine light that these fishermen had never seen before. That revelation impacted Simon Peter in a profound way. In the light of Jesus' glory he saw his own sinfulness, and feared for his life: "Go away from me, Lord; I am a sinful man!" The closer we get to God, the more aware we become not only of His majesty but also of our own unworthiness. Peter knew he was in the presence of holiness and his first response was to try to distance himself. This expression of humility prepared him for the next step: responding to the call of Jesus.

Another significant thing happened on the lake that day. As a result of their obedience Peter, Andrew, James, and John received from Jesus a call to destiny: " 'Don't be afraid; from now on you will catch men.' So they pulled their boats up on shore, left everything and followed Him."

Jesus' call to discipleship and destiny was also an invitation to intimacy. Intimacy with God is another way to describe the abundant life. The Lord is much more interested in our love and devotion than He is in anything that we try to "do" for Him. In fact, the only way we can do anything truly worthwhile for God is if we are first completely devoted to Him, walking in obedience to His will, and living in a continuing and growing intimate love relationship with Him. We always serve God more out of who we are than out of what we do.

Obedience to the Lord is the key to intimacy with Him. First, it is proof of our love. Jesus said, "If you love Me, you will obey what I command" (Jn. 14:15). Second, obedience opens the door to deeper fellowship. When we obey Him we get to know Him better because we learn more about who He is. As we get to know Him better we grow to love Him more, and the more we love Him, the more intimate and personal our relationship with Him becomes. The closer we grow to Christ, the greater fullness and overflowing abundance of life we enjoy.

The writer of Psalm 42 knew from experience what it was to be intimate with God. It begins with a longing hunger for Him.

> As the deer pants for streams of water, so my soul pants for You, O God. My soul thirsts for God, for the living God. When can I go and meet with God?...Deep calls to deep in the roar of Your waterfalls; all Your waves and breakers have swept over me. By day the Lord directs His love, at night His song is with me—a prayer to the God of my life (Psalm 42:1-2,7-8).

In the intimate presence of God, His billows of love wash over us like the waves and breakers of the sea.

One of our biggest problems as believers is that so many of us have a relationship with Christ that is little more than skin deep. We shun the exhilaration of the deep water for the safety of the shallows. God is not satisfied with that; He wants to take us deeper. His purpose in this is not to bless us as much as it is to prepare us for the "catch"—our higher destiny. We must be willing to allow the Lord to take us past our comfort zone with no safety net other than His grace and presence. His goal is for us to become more and more Christlike all the time. The only way we can become like Christ is by knowing Him, and the "deep" is where we find Him. God wants us singing with the whales, not conversing with the goldfish. We cannot do that unless we launch out into the deep.

Many people are scared to death at the thought of that kind of intimate relationship with God, but that's the kind of relationship He is looking for. It is also the only kind in which we will find our greatest purpose and fulfillment. Unless we are willing to submit ourselves to His embrace and enter into that deep and intimately personal relationship with God, we will never get to where He is or where He wants us to be. As a result, we will never accomplish in His Kingdom all that He wants to do in and through us. We will miss the "catch of a lifetime."

Have You Received the Third Kiss?

BERNARD OF CLAIRVAUX (1090-1153) DESCRIBED the journey to intimacy with God using the metaphor of three kisses. The first kiss is the kiss on the feet, which is the action of a servant. It represents repentance. When we first come to the Lord we come to Him as a servant. We bow down before Him and kiss His feet, as it were, which is our way of saying, "I'm not worthy."

The Lord doesn't want us to stay in that position, so He lifts us to the place of the second kiss, the kiss on the hands. This is the kiss of friendship. We know the Lord in a deeper way that a mere servant never can, and have made the deliberate decision to follow Him. Jesus is still our Master, but now He is also our friend.

At some point the day comes when we look into Jesus' eyes and realize that He desires more than just friendship. We suddenly see Him as the Bridegroom of the Song of Solomon, entering His chambers for an intimate interlude with His lover, His bride. Here is the third kiss, the kiss on the lips, the kiss of true intimacy. It represents becoming one in spirit with Christ.

Some people get very uncomfortable visualizing a close relationship with Jesus in such overtly physical images. I don't think anything less vivid can adequately convey to us either the depth of our Lord's love for us or the intensity of His desire for intimate fellowship with us. Besides, God's Word itself speaks of spiritual intimacy using words and imagery that are decidedly sensual in nature:

> *Therefore, you kings, be wise; be warned, you rulers of the earth. Serve the Lord with fear and rejoice with trembling. Kiss the Son, lest He be angry and you be destroyed in your way, for His wrath can flare up in a moment. Blessed are all who take refuge in Him* (Psalm 2:10-12).

> *Let him kiss me with the kisses of his mouth—for your love is more delightful than wine. Pleasing is the fragrance of your perfumes; your name is like perfume poured out. No wonder the maidens love you! Take me away with you—let us hurry! Let the king bring me into his chambers. We rejoice and delight in you; we will praise your love more than wine. How right they are to adore you!* (Song of Solomon 1:2-4)

In these verses from the Song of Solomon, who desires the kiss? The bride. Why? Because she is in love. Hers is a soul thirsting for God. The bride cannot be a slave, who fears her master, or a hireling, who merely desires wages. She cannot be only a disciple, seeking nothing more than knowledge. The bride cannot be a daughter, honoring her parent. She can only be that one who comes to the bridegroom with the desire for complete union with her beloved.

We can think of the third kiss, the kiss on the lips that the bridegroom gives to his bride, as the gift of the Holy Spirit given to us as believers by Christ, our Bridegroom. There is an affection unique to divinity between the Father and the Son, and we are allowed to share equally in that intimacy through the Holy Spirit.

There is a fourth kiss that we must consider and guard against: the kiss on the cheek. This is the kiss of betrayal—the kiss of Judas—the kiss of false intimacy. I believe the thing that hurt Jesus the most on the last night and day before His death was not the ordeal of His trial, or the pain of His beatings, or even the agony of His crucifixion. What hurt Jesus the most was Judas' kiss.

Nothing hurts more than being betrayed by a friend. When someone you love and trust turns on you, it feels like you have been stabbed in the heart. Think about Judas for a minute. Here was a guy who walked with Jesus, talked with Jesus, heard His teachings and saw His miracles, yet still didn't get it. Jesus called Judas, taught him, befriended him, and loved him, and in the end Judas sold Him out for 30 pieces of silver. The symbol of Judas' betrayal was a kiss on Jesus' cheek, a kiss of false intimacy. Judas spent a lot of time with Jesus, but he never really knew Him.

How often are we like Judas in that we put on a good outward display of love and devotion that covers an inward emptiness? We go to church two or three times a week and we sing the songs, but we never step over into that place of real intimacy with God. We never take the time to get to really know Him. If we do not know Jesus we cannot become like Him, and unless we are becoming like Him we cannot fulfill our destiny. Our ultimate destiny as Christians lies not as servants or even friends of Jesus, but as lovers. We are His Bride and He is our Bridegroom.

Where do you stand in your relationship with the Lord? Have you shared with Him the kiss of intimacy, or have you only kissed Him on the cheek?

Intimacy Produces Fruit

IN ORDER TO BECOME LIKE JESUS, we need to bear spiritual fruit in our lives. And in order to bear fruit, we must become intimate with Him. No one gets pregnant at a distance. If we want to become "pregnant" with that which Christ wants to birth in our lives, we must get close to Him. Intimacy results in pregnancy, and pregnancy produces offspring (fruit). When we as believers do not have an intimate relationship with the Lord, it shows in our lives because we do not bear much fruit, and most of what we do bear is small, weak, and sickly. Many of us then try to compensate for our lack of fruit by pointing to all the stuff we *do* for God's Kingdom. Apart from an intimate relationship with Jesus, we cannot do anything worthwhile or lasting for His Kingdom. All we will do is die on the vine.

On the night before He died, Jesus taught His disciples an important lesson about intimacy. As He frequently did on other occasions, Jesus used a metaphor from horticulture to impart a divine truth.

> *I am the true vine, and My Father is the gardener. He cuts off every branch in Me that bears no fruit, while every branch that does bear fruit He prunes so that it will be even more fruitful. You are already clean because of the word I have spoken to you. Remain in me, and I will remain in you. No branch can bear fruit by itself; it must remain in the vine. Neither can you bear fruit unless you remain in Me. I am the vine; you are the branches. If a man remains in Me and I in him, he will bear much fruit;*

apart from Me you can do nothing. If anyone does not remain in Me, he is like a branch that is thrown away and withers; such branches are picked up, thrown into the fire and burned. If you remain in Me and My words remain in you, ask whatever you wish, and it will be given you. This is to My Father's glory, that you bear much fruit, showing yourselves to be My disciples (John 15:1-8).

Jesus is the vine and we are the branches. Branches do not produce fruit; they simply bear the fruit produced in and by the vine. Any branch that is separated from the vine shrivels and dies, becoming totally useless. A branch can do nothing by itself.

In the same way, our fruitfulness depends on our remaining intimately connected to Jesus, our Vine. The word "remain" in these verses is a translation of the Greek word *meno*, which literally means "to stay" or "abide." It carries the idea of a continuing state of dwelling rather than a temporary condition. To "remain" in Jesus means to dwell continually with Him in a permanent state of fellowship and rest.

Jesus promised that when we abide in Him we will "bear much fruit." This will bring glory to the Father because our fruitfulness will show the world that we are disciples of Christ. When we bear fruit we prove to the world both the reality of God and the truth of the gospel. Bearing fruit means that we grow in Christlike graces and the fruit of the Spirit: love, joy, peace, patience, kindness, goodness, faithfulness, gentleness, and self-control (see Gal. 5:22).

Intimacy with God brings another benefit beyond spiritual fruit and maturity: a deep and loving friendship with One to whom we can open our hearts and bare our deepest thoughts and feelings. Francois Fenelon, a 17th-century French archbishop and theologian, beautifully described the warm and personal nature of this communion with our Lord:

> Tell God all that is in your heart, as one unloads one's heart, its pleasures and its pains, to a dear friend. Tell Him your troubles, that He may comfort you; tell Him your joys, that He may sober them; tell Him your longings, that He may purify them; tell Him your dislikes, that He may help you to conquer them; talk to Him of your temptations, that He may shield you from them; show Him the wounds of your heart, that He may heal them; lay bare your indifference to good, your depraved tastes for evil, your instability. Tell Him how self-love makes you unjust to others, how vanity tempts you to be insincere, how pride disguises you to yourself as to others.
>
> If you thus pour out all your weaknesses, needs, troubles, there will be no lack of what to say. You will never exhaust the subject. It is continually being renewed. People who have no secrets from each other never want subjects of conversation. They do not weigh their words, for there is nothing to be held back; neither do they seek for something to say. They talk out of the abundance of the heart, without consideration, just what they think. Blessed are they who attain to such familiar, unreserved intercourse with God.

When All Else Fails, We Still Have Jesus

HOW DO WE GET TO THE PLACE of such sweet and close communion with the Lord? The same way we achieve intimacy with anyone—by yielding to Him. Yielding is related to obedience, but softer in tone. Obedience often suggests a master-slave relationship. Yielding, on the other hand, is a characteristic of a love relationship because it involves willing submission on our part. We may obey out of duty, but we yield out of love.

God is constantly wooing us through His Word and through His Spirit, always inviting us into intimate relationship with Him. Many times we resist because we are afraid of being hurt. Becoming intimate with someone means making ourselves vulnerable. That can be dangerous. We have learned from bitter experience in the world that whenever we make ourselves vulnerable there is always someone nearby who is ready to nail us to the wall.

Unlike the world, God will never abuse our trust. He will not use us for His own desires and then toss us out like yesterday's garbage. He invites us to open ourselves up—to yield or surrender ourselves—and enter into close personal communion with Him. For many of us, that's a scary thought. It gets right back to the issue of operating without a safety net. If we are going to follow Jesus we have to realize that there will be people who want to crucify us just like they crucified Him. Whenever we identify ourselves with Jesus we become targets for His enemies. Identifying personally and intimately with Jesus is the only way we will ever fulfill the destiny He has for us. It is the only way we will ever get to where God wants us to be.

When you get right down to it, the only thing in life that is really important is knowing Jesus. That's why we need to learn to yield ourselves willingly to an intimate relationship with Him. Even if we lose everything and everyone else, as long as we have Jesus we have all we need. Thomas à Kempis, in his classic 15th-century work *The Imitation of Christ*, wrote:

> Give to Christ, therefore, free entrance into your heart, and keep out all things that withstand His

entrance. When you have Him, you are rich enough, and He alone will be sufficient to you. Then He will be your provider and defender and your faithful helper in every necessity. So that you will not need to put your trust in any other save Him.

When we walk in a growing relationship of intimacy with Jesus, we discover that our vulnerability is covered by His strength and peace. Because we are abiding with Him as a branch abides in the vine, the attacks of others do not bother us as much as they used to. As Thomas à Kempis writes, "Moreover, a man who is well ordered in his soul heeds little the unkind and proud behavior of worldly people."

Sometimes we have to lose everything to discover what's truly important. That's what happened to me. When it was all stripped away—my fame, my fortune, my success as a Christian comedian, my self-esteem—I found that Jesus was still there. While everything else vanished, I still had my relationship with the Lord. Somehow amid all the distraction and confusion and misplaced priorities of my life the kernel of intimate fellowship with Jesus remained. In the wreckage of all that I had built, it shone brightly like a precious jewel.

That relationship sustained me even through the worst of everything I endured, after I crashed and burned, and during my restoration. It gave me the ability to step onto the back porch that cold night and cry out, "You know!" I drew so much comfort just in the knowledge that He had saved me and done so much else for me. I knew what I was, and what I had been. I saw myself as Jesus saw me—as His precious friend—and knew He loved me in spite of everything. That realization filled me with an overwhelming sense of gratitude and thanksgiving. Suddenly, nothing else I had ever been or done counted for anything. Knowing Jesus was all that mattered.

My experience helped me identify personally with Paul's perspective, which he described to the Philippians:

But whatever was to my profit I now consider loss for the sake of Christ. What is more, I consider everything a loss compared to the surpassing greatness of knowing Christ Jesus my Lord, for whose sake I have lost all things. I consider them rubbish, that I may gain Christ and be found in Him, not having a righteousness of my own that comes from the law, but that which is through faith in Christ— the righteousness that comes from God and is by faith. I want to know Christ and the power of His resurrection and the fellowship of sharing in His sufferings, becoming like Him in His death, and so, somehow, to attain to the resurrection from the dead. Not that I have already obtained all this, or have already been made perfect, but I press on to take hold of that for which Christ Jesus took hold of me. Brothers, I do not consider myself yet to have taken hold of it. But one thing I do: Forgetting what is behind and straining toward what is ahead, I press on toward the goal to win the prize for which God has called me heavenward in Christ Jesus (Philippians 3:7-14).

Our Ultimate Purpose Is to Know Jesus

DON'T LET WHAT *USED* TO BE KEEP YOU from pressing ahead to what *can* be. The past is the past. Nothing matters except knowing Jesus and walking in His will and purpose. His invitation to intimacy is always open. Most of us have never done anything more than to skim the surface of our relationship with the Lord. It is time to launch out into the deep—to plumb the unfathomable depths of His love, grace, mercy, and communion. Open your arms and dive in. Embrace Him; He stands ready with arms open to embrace you.

An anonymous author had this to say regarding what we are about as believers:

> Purpose to seek Him—He will always be your reward.
>
> Purpose to know Him—He will always reveal Himself to you.
>
> Purpose to follow Him—He will always lead the way.
>
> Purpose to enjoy Him—He will always be your dearest friend.
>
> Purpose to praise Him—He will always be the worthy one.
>
> Purpose to trust Him—He will always be your faithful provider.
>
> Purpose to please Him—He will always give you what is good.
>
> Purpose to be totally His—He will always be totally yours!

Ultimately, the secret to intimacy with the Lord is found in continually yielding to Him: listening to His soft voice and His gentle wooing, and surrendering in willful submission to His loving embrace. In order to hear His voice consistently we need to spend regular time with Him in prayer, in reading His Word, and in quiet fellowship.

This kind of intimacy requires on our part unconditional surrender to the will of God; what Oswald Chambers calls "my utmost for His highest—my best for His glory." He goes on to say, "To reach that level of determination is a matter of the will, not of debate or of reasoning. It is absolute and irrevocable surrender of the will at that point....Shut out every other thought and keep yourself before God in this one thing only—my utmost for His highest. I am determined to be absolutely and entirely for Him and Him alone."[1]

Such total and absolute surrender is at the heart of this prayer by an unknown author:

> My God, I am not my own but yours. Take me for your own, and help me in all things to do your holy will. My God, I give myself to you, in joy and sorrow, in sickness and in health, in success and in failure, in life and in death, in time and for eternity. Make me and keep me your own, through Jesus Christ our Lord. Amen.

ENDNOTE

1. Oswald Chambers, *My Utmost For His Highest*, devotional for January 1, Copyright © 1992 by Oswald Chambers Publications Association, Ltd. Original edition copyright © 1935 by Dodd, Mead & Company, Inc. Copyright renewed 1963 by Oswald Chambers Publications Association, Ltd. All Rights reserved. United States publication rights are held by Discovery House Publishers, which is affiliated with RBC Ministries, Grand Rapids, Michigan 49512. Electronic Edition STEP Files Copyright © 1998, Parsons Technology, Inc., all rights reserved.

Chapter Nine

WHAT'S THAT IDOL DOING THERE?

We are not destined to happiness,
nor to health, but to holiness.[1]
—*Oswald Chambers*

NATHANIEL HAWTHORNE'S CLASSIC SHORT STORY "The Birthmark" tells of a young scientist named Aylmer whose fixation on his wife Georgiana's one physical flaw—a tiny birthmark on her left cheek—prevents him from loving and appreciating her as she is. In Aylmer's mind, the blemish represents unacceptable imperfection in his wife that overshadows her true beauty of body and spirit:

> In this manner, selecting it as the symbol of his wife's liability to sin, sorrow, decay, and death, Aylmer's somber imagination was not long in rendering the birthmark a frightful object, causing him more trouble and horror than ever Georgiana's beauty, whether of soul or sense, had given him delight.[2]

Aylmer's obsession with eliminating his wife's "defect" leads to disaster. His compulsive preoccupation rubs off on Georgiana until she hates her birthmark more than he does and is willing to undergo any treatment to get rid of it. Aylmer uses his scientific expertise to prepare a special concoction for her to drink. In the end he succeeds, but at tragic cost. The same elixir that removes Georgiana's birthmark also poisons her to death.

Many people in the Body of Christ often resemble Aylmer in their attitudes and actions toward other believers. None of us are necessarily immune. We can become so focused on a person's flaws that we lose sight of that person's strengths, positive qualities, and inner beauty. One mistake, one slip-up, one lapse in judgment, one sin, and we're ready to crucify. Others are just as quick to nail *us* when *we* screw up.

Much of the interpersonal and interdenominational strife in the Church today is the result of a judgmental spirit on the part of believers toward one another. Our sinful nature makes us prone to criticize and judge others as a means of lifting ourselves up. Let's be honest: Deep down inside, most of us are convinced that anyone who disagrees with us is wrong. If we're not careful, attitudes that we may not even be conscious of can lead us to be intolerant of the perceived weaknesses of others.

One of the most common sources of disagreement is differing perceptions of how to live the Christian life. Many of the victims of "friendly fire" are people who have run afoul of somebody else's concept of holiness.

For some reason a lot of us have perceived the idea that holiness is all about externals: Dress right, walk right, talk right, wear the right hairstyle, get rid of the makeup, toe the line, obey all the rules, and on and on. These things may present a very pleasing and impressive appearance on the outside, but hide a cold, worldly, and unchanged heart on the inside. This is just what Jesus was talking about in Matthew 23:27

when He described the teachers of the law and the Pharisees as "whitewashed tombs, which look beautiful on the outside but on the inside are full of dead men's bones and everything unclean." By all appearances they were righteous men—the cream of the crop—but it was all show.

True holiness has nothing to do with adhering to man-made rules or expectations, but everything to do with abandoned obedience to God.

Holiness Grows From the Inside Out

WHEN CHRIST CALLED US to salvation through repentance and faith in Him as Savior and Lord, He also called us to a life of holiness. Holy living is at the core of everything we are and do as believers. Simon Peter wrote, "But just as He who called you is holy, so be holy in all you do; for it is written: 'Be holy, because I am holy' " (1 Pet. 1:15-16). In a way, Peter is saying, "Like Father, like son (or daughter)." God is our Father, and He is holy. As His children we should bear the family resemblance.

One way to describe holiness is to say that it is the process of becoming like Jesus. Holiness must be inward before it can be outward. Holiness begins in our hearts when we receive Christ as our Savior and Lord. The Holy Spirit comes in and starts to work on our hearts, changing and conforming us into the image and likeness of Christ. Those heart changes manifest themselves outwardly as changes in our attitudes, our speech, our appearance, and our behavior.

The more we yield ourselves to the Spirit's work in us, the better we come to know Christ and the more like Him we become. William Penn wrote, "As man becomes holy, just, merciful, patient...by the copy he will know the original, and by the workmanship in himself he will be acquainted with the holy workman."[3]

Paul certainly understood the difference between internal and external holiness. Raised as a strict Jew, he learned early the significance of circumcision as the outward evidence that identified Jews as the special covenant people of God. Circumcision was an external sign of holiness signifying that the Jews were a people set apart for the Lord. On the other hand, as a follower of Christ Paul came to understand through the Holy Spirit that physical, outward circumcision was not enough.

> *Circumcision has value if you observe the law, but if you break the law, you have become as though you had not been circumcised. If those who are not circumcised keep the law's requirements, will they not be regarded as though they were circumcised? The one who is not circumcised physically and yet obeys the law will condemn you who, even though you have the written code and circumcision, are a lawbreaker. A man is not a Jew if he is only one outwardly, nor is circumcision merely outward and physical. No, a man is a Jew if he is one inwardly; and circumcision is circumcision of the heart, by the Spirit, not by the written code. Such a man's praise is not from men, but from God* (Romans 2:25-29).

Paul is saying external religious observances mean nothing if our hearts have not been changed. They have value only if they grow out of inward holiness. Those whose hearts have been "circumcised"—made holy by the Spirit of Christ—look not to other people but to God for their validation. God accepts them on that basis, not on the basis of their religious exercises.

Romans 12:2 says that we are to be transformed by the renewing of our minds. How does that happen? The moment we accept Christ as our Savior and Lord, His Spirit comes to live permanently in our hearts. He cleanses our sins with His blood and makes us holy. In practical terms, the working out of that holiness in our everyday lives is a process that grows over time. As we live in God's Word and walk in what we have experienced in our hearts, we begin to filter those things through our minds. The Holy Spirit reveals to us what attitudes and behavior are appropriate and inappropriate for our relationship with Jesus, and as we yield to Him our inner transformation is manifested more and more in our outward behavior.

God is interested in our hearts, not our outward appearance. His purpose is to conform us to the image and likeness of His Son, which means cutting away everything in our lives that is contrary to that image. It is said that when the great Italian sculptor Michelangelo prepared to carve a statue he first envisioned in his mind the completed sculpture, then simply chipped away from the marble everything that did not conform to his mental picture.

The Holy Spirit works in a similar manner, showing us the things in our lives that do not conform to the image of Christ. He urges us to deal with them, but He never forces us to obey. The final decision is up to us. That's why each of us will manifest our holiness differently. We will not all look the same or dress the same. Some of us will have long hair, while others will have short hair. With surgical precision, the Spirit targets anything that holds us back from becoming like Jesus or from following Him wholeheartedly. Holiness means getting rid of anything that stands between us and Jesus. It means pulling down all the idols in our lives.

Holiness Is Pulling Down All the Idols in Our Lives

AFTER THE DEATH OF KING SOLOMON, David's son, the nation of Israel split into two separate kingdoms.

147

Ten of the tribes rebelled against Solomon's son and successor, Rehoboam, and formed the northern kingdom of Israel. The other two tribes, Judah and Benjamin, remained loyal to David's line and established the southern kingdom of Judah.

Out of all the kings of Judah, Manasseh was probably the worst. Under Manasseh's rule the people of Judah degenerated into the grossest forms of idolatry and pagan worship. Pagan altars, Asherah poles, and other idols were everywhere. Idolatrous worship including sexual immorality and human sacrifice was a blight on the land. The sins of Manasseh were so great that God's judgment on Judah became inevitable and irreversible. Manasseh's son Amon was not much better than his father. Then came Josiah.

Josiah was different. Although he was Manasseh's grandson, he did not follow his grandfather's example. Ascending the throne at the age of eight, Josiah began earnestly seeking the Lord when he was sixteen. Second Chronicles 34:2 says of Josiah: "He did what was right in the eyes of the Lord and walked in the ways of his father David, not turning aside to the right or to the left."

When Josiah was 20 he embarked on an aggressive campaign to rid the land of idolatry and turn the people back to the Lord. He repaired the Temple in Jerusalem, which had been neglected for many years. He destroyed all the pagan altars and Asherah poles, as well as all the pagan worship groves, including those on the "high places." He put to death all the pagan priests and priestesses. Because his heart was turned to the Lord, Josiah was determined to purge from the land all idolatry and all that was unholy. In this he was more thorough than any of his predecessors since his ancestor, King David.

Josiah's example is a good illustration of what it means to pursue holiness. Exodus 20:5 says that the Lord is a "jealous"

God; He will brook no rivals. Anything in our lives that competes with God for our love, loyalty, and allegiance is dangerous to our spiritual welfare and needs either to be brought under submission or eliminated.

Paul addressed this issue in his second letter to the Corinthian Christians, who were struggling with that very problem:

> What agreement is there between the temple of God and idols? For we are the temple of the living God. As God has said: "I will live with them and walk among them, and I will be their God, and they will be My people. Therefore come out from them and be separate, says the Lord. Touch no unclean thing, and I will receive you. I will be a Father to you, and you will be My sons and daughters, says the Lord Almighty." Since we have these promises, dear friends, let us purify ourselves from everything that contaminates body and spirit, perfecting holiness out of reverence for God (2 Corinthians 6:16-7:1).

Unholy thoughts, habits, words, and behavior are incompatible with the lifestyles of people who have been made holy through the blood of Christ. We need to separate ourselves from anything and everything that is ungodly in our lives. We need to pull down all our idols.

Whatever Your Particular Idol Is, Destroy It

BY PULLING DOWN OUR IDOLS I'm not necessarily talking only about sinful or evil things. Some things that are not wrong in and of themselves may be wrong for us if they capture first place in our hearts.

Because each of us is different, the specific things we deal with in order to grow in personal holiness will often be different as well. Something that is a problem for me may not be a problem for you, and vice versa. There are, of course, some general things that we all must do in order to become Christians and grow in the Lord: Trust Christ as our Savior, develop habits of Bible study and prayer, be active in a local church, walk in the Spirit, abstain from sexual immorality, etc. There are also specific things that God will speak to us about individually that involve our personal holiness. They may relate to a bad habit we need to give up, or our attitude toward material possessions, or a personal prejudice, or any number of other things. At any rate, God will reveal these things to us and consequently it is our responsibility to obey Him and deal with those things He shows us. Obedience is the key to growth in holiness.

Not too long ago, I wrote this prayer about submission to the will of God:

Forgive me my Father, Brother and Friend—sweet Holy Spirit; for not trusting You more fully. Please do not allow me to become a tourist in the House of the Lord. Seed in me that which will produce good fruit. Cast about me Your hedge of protection to keep the enemy out and my restless spirit in. May I strive to submit to You perfectly so that my delight in You will be perfect too. Help me not to transgress Your law of love. May I love those that deserve it and those that don't even more. Let me see Your face, not situations, problems, or challenges, but Your face alone. Pass me in at the gate of Your sheepfold. Keep me by Your staff and rod. I do not want to be a tourist in the House of the Lord.

One day Jesus was approached by a young man who had a serious spiritual question. Wasting no time, the man cut right to the chase:

Now a man came up to Jesus and asked, "Teacher, what good thing must I do to get eternal life?" "Why

*do you ask Me about what is good?" Jesus replied.
"There is only One who is good. If you want to enter
life, obey the commandments." "Which ones?" the
man inquired. Jesus replied, " 'Do not murder, do
not commit adultery, do not steal, do not give false
testimony, honor your father and mother,' and 'love
your neighbor as yourself.' " "All these I have kept,"
the young man said. "What do I still lack?" Jesus
answered, "If you want to be perfect, go, sell your
possessions and give to the poor, and you will have
treasure in heaven. Then come, follow Me." When
the young man heard this, he went away sad,
because he had great wealth* (Matthew 19:16-22).

This is the only instance in the New Testament where
Jesus specifically tells someone to give up his wealth. Nevertheless, there have been believers in every generation who
have tried to turn this into a "one size fits all" doctrine that
says that anyone who *really* wants to follow Christ must take
a vow of poverty. This misses the point entirely. By all
accounts, Nicodemus was wealthy, and so was Joseph of Ari-
mathea, yet there is no indication in the Bible that Jesus ever
challenged either of them to give up his wealth.

The issue is not whether it is right or wrong for a person
to be wealthy. In and of itself, wealth is neutral. Jesus told the
young man to part with his wealth not because it was wrong to
be rich, but because his riches had become his god. This young
man's wealth was his hang-up, the idol that prevented him
from following Christ. Before he could inherit eternal life;
before he could become holy in God's sight, that particular
idol had to come down.

In the end, the young man could not do it. He could not
part with his possessions. Following Jesus came at a cost he
was not willing to pay, so "he went away sad."

We serve an iconoclastic God; He hates idolatry and false images. If we are going to be serious about following the Lord and pursuing holiness, we need to understand that He is serious about pulling down and destroying all the idols in our lives. God will not share His glory with another. As believers, we are children of God, and He demands absolute first place in our lives. Whatever your particular idol may be, destroy it. Holiness means no idols; we are to love and serve the Lord and Him alone.

We Grow in Holiness as We Grow in Love

IF WE REALLY LOVE SOMEONE, we are willing to do almost anything for that person as a demonstration of our love. If we see something in our life that hinders the growth of our love relationship with that person, we are quick to take care of it. As our love grows, so does our desire to be rid of anything that keeps us from being as close as possible to the one we love.

God loves us and wants us to be close to Him. He has called us to be holy just as He is holy. The only problem is that we are unholy people because of our sinful nature. If we are to draw near to the Lord and become holy in the most practical sense, then we must somehow deal with our sin. Within ourselves we do not possess the power for holiness; it must come from God. Fortunately for us, God has provided that power. In Christ we have been given all things. Nothing stands in the way of our growing in holiness, except perhaps our own pride or disobedience. God has given us the power to be holy, but it is up to us to make it happen. He can show us the way, but we have to step out and walk that path.

Simon Peter described the process of growing in holiness this way:

His divine power has given us everything we need for life and godliness through our knowledge of Him who called us by His own glory and goodness. Through these He has given us His very great and precious promises, so that through them you may participate in the divine nature and escape the corruption in the world caused by evil desires. For this very reason, make every effort to add to your faith goodness; and to goodness, knowledge; and to knowledge, self-control; and to self-control, perseverance; and to perseverance, godliness; and to godliness, brotherly kindness; and to brotherly kindness, love. For if you possess these qualities in increasing measure, they will keep you from being ineffective and unproductive in your knowledge of our Lord Jesus Christ (2 Peter 1:3-8).

Practical holiness is a progression of growth from faith to love; from conversion to maturity. When we place our faith in Christ to save us, He builds goodness in us by coming to dwell in our hearts, where He begins to smooth out our rough edges and soften our spirit. We become more sensitive and responsive to His presence, which leads us to greater knowledge, not only of Him but also of ourselves and the negative and unholy qualities we need to remove. As our desire to be like Jesus grows, so does our desire to be free of anything that hinders us. We learn to deal with those things through self-control. Exercising self-control teaches us to persevere under pressure and temptation. Perseverance builds godly character. The more godly we are, the more loving we are, first to our brothers and sisters in Christ, and then to all people.

We see this happen all the time. It is one of the miracles of God's grace. Let's say some guy who is a drunk or a druggie gets saved. Maybe for a little while at first he still drinks some or still does dope, but as the Lord really gets hold of his life he begins to change. Pretty soon he realizes he needs to give up the booze and the dope, and goes through the process of sobering up and getting clean. He starts taking greater pride in himself. Then one day he shows up at church in something other than a ragged T-shirt and torn blue jeans. Before long he is volunteering for some ministry or to lead a small group Bible study. Maybe he even joins the choir. Eventually he meets a beautiful Christian young woman and they get married and have children. Ten years down the line, none who meet him would imagine in their wildest dreams that he was once a boozer and a junkie.

Despite my long hair and earrings, many people are still amazed when I share with them about my past involvement with satanism, the occult, and drugs. It simply blows them away. They say to me, "I just can't imagine you doing any of that." The reason I am so different now from the way I used to be is because Jesus wrought a change in my life. It didn't happen overnight, but developed over time.

Holiness outwardly manifests itself differently in different people, but produces the same end result in every believer: Christlikeness. It begins with a heart relationship with the Lord and grows to the point where the holiness of God has become so much a part of us that people who knew us before we were saved would hardly recognize us now. We have become like Jesus. That's what true holiness is.

Healthy Holiness Calls for the Right Diet

I OFTEN TELL PEOPLE that there are four ingredients needed in order for us to be healthy believers. The first is food. We must feed on a regular and steady diet of the Word of God. It is bread for our souls. God's Word nourishes our spirits like meat, fruit, and vegetables nourish our bodies.

We receive God's Word in two ways: through the Bible and through personal revelation. The Bible is paramount; it is the standard by which everything else must be measured. Personal revelation is secondary to the Bible. In order to make sure our personal revelation is not screwy and leads us off in weird directions, we must evaluate it by the Bible. We are okay to proceed only if our personal revelation lines up with the written Word of God. Otherwise, we need to reexamine and ask the Lord for clarification.

The second ingredient for healthy holiness is faith. I don't mean our initial "saving faith" when we first come to Christ, but the day-by-day walk of faith where we share with other people, by word as well as deed, what the Lord has done and is doing in our lives. Witnessing for Christ exercises our faith the way physical training exercises our bodies. The more we share our faith with others, the stronger and more real it becomes to us.

In addition to spiritual food and faith, we need fellowship with other believers to grow a healthy and holy life. Some people insist, "I can be a Christian without going to church." True. We could also climb Mount Everest in our underwear. The problem is that we would be in danger of freezing to death in both places. As believers, we need *koinonia*, that warm fellowship through which we learn and grow, give and receive encouragement. *Koinonia* provides a warm and secure shelter for our spirit just as a house does for our body.

Finally, for healthy holiness, we need the element of regular prayer. It's impossible to have a healthy relationship with someone we never talk to. If God's Word is the bread, then prayer is the water. Both are essential for life.

William Longstaff, a 19th-century hymn writer, penned a hymn that speaks to all of these elements of holiness:

Take time to be holy, speak oft with thy Lord;
Abide in Him always, and feed on His Word;
Make friends of God's children, help those who are weak;
Forgetting in nothing His blessing to seek.
Take time to be holy, the world rushes on;
Spend much time in secret with Jesus alone;
By looking to Jesus like Him thou shalt be;
Thy friends in thy conduct His likeness shall see.
Take time to be holy, let Him be thy guide;
And run not before Him whatever betide;
In joy or in sorrow still follow thy Lord,
And looking to Jesus, still trust in His Word.
Take time to be holy, be calm in thy soul;
Each thought and each motive beneath His control;
Thus led by His Spirit to fountains of love,
Thou soon shalt be fitted for service above.

In the final analysis, holiness is very personal in nature. As we yield to Him, the Lord leads each of us into a place of obedience to His will. His objective (and ours) is that our hearts and minds should be pure and filled with love for Him alone, a love that permeates us, body and spirit, motivates us in everything we do and say, and inspires us to become all that God desires us to be. The spirit of this desire is captured beautifully in this hymn/prayer written in 1653 by Paul Gerhardt, a German hymnist, and translated into English by John Wesley:

Jesus, Thy boundless love to me
No thought can reach, no tongue declare;
O bind my thankful heart to Thee,
And reign without a rival there:
Thine wholly, Thine alone, I am;
Be Thou alone my constant flame.
O grant that nothing in my soul
May dwell but Thy pure love alone;
O may Thy love possess me whole,
My joy, my treasure, and my crown:
All coldness from my heart remove;

May ev'ry act, word, thought, be love.
O Love, how gracious is Thy way!
All fear before Thy presence flies;
Care, anguish, sorrow melt away,
Where'er Thy healing beams arise:
O Jesus, nothing may I see,
Nothing desire, or seek, but Thee.
In suff'ring be Thy love my peace;
In weakness, be Thy love my power;
And when the storms of life shall cease,
O Jesus, in that solemn hour,
In death as life be Thou my guide,
And save me, who for me hast died.

ENDNOTES

1. Oswald Chambers, *My Utmost For His Highest*, devotional for September 1, Copyright © 1992 by Oswald Chambers Publications Association, Ltd. Original edition copyright © 1935 by Dodd, Mead & Company, Inc. Copyright renewed 1963 by Oswald Chambers Publications Association, Ltd. All Rights reserved. United States publication rights are held by Discovery House Publishers, which is affiliated with RBC Ministries, Grand Rapids, Michigan 49512. Electronic Edition STEP Files Copyright © 1998, Parsons Technology, Inc., all rights reserved.

2. Nathaniel Hawthorne, "The Birthmark," *The Complete Novels and Selected Tales of Nathaniel Hawthorne*, Norman Holmes Pearson, ed., Modern Library Edition. (New York: Random House, Inc., 1937), 1022.

3. William Penn, quoted in *Classics Devotional Bible*, NIV (Grand Rapids, MI: Zondervan Publishing House, 1996), 1458.

Chapter Ten

YOU'RE NEVER TOO FAR GONE TO COME BACK

Just as I am, Thou wilt receive...
O Lamb of God, I come!
—*Charlotte Elliot*

YEARS AGO, WHEN THE CONTROVERSY over my earlier ministry was still hot, I was attending the annual convention of the Christian Booksellers Association when a man approached me loaded for bear. He had fire in his eyes and I could practically see the smoke coming out of his ears. Instinctively, I braced myself for a confrontation. Getting right in my face, he let loose with both barrels.

"How could you dare to show your face around here after what you did? You're an absolute disgrace to the Body of Christ. You're not worthy to breathe the same air as the rest of the Christians here."

Although my accuser was a Christian brother, this was not a godly confrontation. He was thoroughly steamed. Anger controlled his words and demeanor. The only thing he wanted to do was rebuke me and put me in my place.

As I stood there absorbing his verbal assault, every fiber in my being pulled at me to jump in with both feet and have it out with the guy right there on the CBA convention floor. I've always had trouble walking away from a fight. It must be the Marine in me. Fortunately, the controversy had forced me to start taking a hard look at myself. In the midst of everything the Lord had already begun working on my pride and my pugnacious tendencies. Before I could lash out at my attacker, something in my brain said, "Pull this dragon's teeth right now!"

I looked my accuser in the eye and simply said, "Sir, you are absolutely right. You've rebuked me, now restore me." He obviously was not expecting such a meek response. It was like I had poked him with a pin. All the anger and fight drained out of him like air hissing from a balloon. He just stood there for a few moments, not knowing what to say, then turned and retreated.

This encounter illustrates at least two truths I discovered about the process of restoration. First, my restoration could not begin until I was ready to accept responsibility for my own actions, failures, and mistakes. The second thing I learned was that plenty of people were ready to criticize, condemn, and rebuke me, but few were willing to get personally involved in helping me to recover. It's always easier to point out someone else's mistakes than it is to help correct them.

God's Grace Is Always Sufficient

MY ROAD TO RECOVERY over the last ten years has been long and bumpy, but I wouldn't take a million dollars in exchange for what I have learned or how I have grown. At the same time, however, I wouldn't give a nickel to go through those experiences again. By the grace of God I have come to the place of being able to thank Him for all I have been through. I have reached a new level of understanding the words of the apostle Paul when he wrote, "Be joyful always; pray continually; give thanks in all circumstances, for this is God's will for you in Christ Jesus" (1 Thess. 5:16-18).

As I look back over the last 30 years of my life, one fact shines out more than anything else: the unfailing goodness of God. After everything that has happened to me, it still comes back to that. God was good when He saved me. He was good as He used me in ministry. He was good even when I wasn't. God was good when He restored me to right fellowship with Him, and He continues to be good as I walk with Him today. God is good all the time. I probably love Him more right now than at any other time in my entire life.

I have read a great deal about grace over the past few years. There is nothing like a great personal need to whet your appetite. When the mob is at the drawbridge howling for your blood, God's grace had *better* be sufficient for all your needs, because at a time like that His grace is all you have left! When you have to throw yourself on the mercy of God, it's good to know that you have someplace to land. Brokenness is a very scary thing. Without the mercy and grace of God there is no hope for one who is broken. Without the Lord, brokenness leads only to despair. With Him, however, brokenness produces both depth and character.

During the blackest of those black days when I was experiencing so many personal attacks, I discovered a song called "Broken Places," by the contemporary gospel group *First Call*. Some of the words of that song are, "He knows the broken places...He heals them one by one..." I can remember sitting in my room and playing that song over and over as I cried my eyes out. It wasn't self-pity that caused my tears to flow, although God knows I have had my battles with that. What made me cry as I listened to that song was knowing that God knew everything about me and about what was going on, and He loved me anyway. Knowing that He did not want to destroy and discard me, but to heal and restore me, literally took my breath away! It was so healing to my spirit just to *hear* about the healing, and to be reminded that I didn't have to go through my "dark night of the soul" alone. I discovered that when God promised, "I will never leave you nor forsake you" (Josh. 1:5), He meant just what He said.

Even when it seemed as though my whole world had come to an end, I knew that God loved me. I also knew that He knew that I loved Him. He knew it on that cold morning when I stood on my back porch and cried out to Him. "You know," I prayed. "No matter what anyone says, You know. No matter what people believe, You know. Please, Lord, look past all my faults and see my heart, because I know You know." God knew that when push came to shove I still wanted to serve Him. He knew that even though I had failed Him miserably, I was willing to do anything He asked. He knew that I was truly sorry for all my sins and mistakes and that I was ready to lay aside all my "wrongness" for a right relationship with Him. That's when His grace kicked in. That's when His mercy took hold. That's when my healing and restoration began.

My Recovery Meant Learning Some Hard Lessons

ONE OF THE FIRST THINGS I had to learn was to take responsibility for the messes I had made. One of our greatest temptations during times of trouble is to try to justify ourselves by pointing our finger at the mistakes of others. "It's her fault, not mine!" "It wasn't me, it was them!" Thanks to the Holy Spirit and the wise counsel of my board of spiritual overseers, this was a fight I was never allowed to make. Silence! That's what they told me. Silence and submission! Oh, man! That meant I had to shut up and do what I was told! That might not be so hard for some people, but it was a real head-buster for me. I wanted to take names! I wanted to leave a trail of destruction that would have made Sherman's march to the sea look like a Sunday school picnic! I had no desire to mount a reasonable defense. All I wanted to do was hurt those who were hurting me.

I thank God that from the start He surrounded me with godly men who helped me understand that once I started down the road of self-defense and self-justification, there would be no coming back. Once we start talking about ourselves and our troubles and how we have been wronged by everyone, we have nothing left to say about Jesus. My problem was that I was too self-centered to begin with. To take the tack of justifying myself would simply be to trade one form of self-indulgence for another. That is *not* what God had in mind.

A second lesson I learned was about humility. It's quite a shock to find out that you're not "all that and a bag of chips" after all. For a long time fame and success isolated me from reality. Because I had money and was on everybody's "short list" of people to know, I thought I was some kind of special breed. I began to think that the rules didn't apply to me, that I could play fast and loose with the things of God because I was under special circumstances.

Once, after a particularly successful concert in Anaheim, California, I was looking at the bag full of offering money and feeling really smug. I had just performed before thousands of people, and the offering was substantial. The audience had shouted for me before I went on, and really went wild when I hit the stage. At the end, I received a standing ovation and five curtain calls. There had also been a large response to the altar call. In that heady atmosphere of success, I said to God, "Lord, if I'm doing something wrong, this is *not* the way to show me!" So, He showed me!

He showed me that no matter what men think, we all must still answer to God. He showed me that no matter how big we get, we still have to play by the rules. I found out that the Lord is not mocked. When you stand toe to toe with the Almighty and say, "Show me," the resulting lesson might just slap your ears down around your ankles. There is nothing like being taken down a peg or two to get you to see Jesus in proper perspective. Glory, honor, blessing, and power belong to the Ancient of Days, not to me and not to you. I learned that there is a price to pay for touching the "consecrated" things.

The third thing I had to learn is that "obedience is better than sacrifice" (see 1 Sam. 15:22). No matter how good something may be that we are doing, or how good we are at doing it, if it is not what the Lord wants us to do, it doesn't amount to much. During all those years when I was out of order, I know the Lord still worked through me. I truly loved the people whom I ministered to, and that was enough for the Holy Spirit to use. However, I became enamored with my career. I was Mike Warnke, America's number-one Christian comedian. The only problem was that God never called me to be America's number-one Christian comedian. He called me to be a minister of the gospel; p. s., I'm funny. My career overtook my calling.

Being funny is part of who I am. The Lord used my comedy then and He still uses it today. Comedy is a tool, but it is not what I "do." Proclaiming the gospel of Jesus Christ is what I do. Humor is a means I use to that end. For a long time I lost sight of that. I became more concerned with my career than with what God had called me to do. As a result, my priorities got all out of whack.

A large part of my restoration process has been getting the cart back behind the horse. I have spent much time in prayer about where God wants me to be and what He wants me to do. Thanks to the prayers of my wife, Susan, and the wise guidance of my spiritual overseers, I believe that I am more directly in God's will today than ever before. My earlier ministry was built on sand. Now, Jesus and His Word are the only "rock" I ever want to build on. It's like the old gospel hymn says, "Trust and obey, for there's no other way to be happy in Jesus, but to trust and obey."

Finally, I had to learn not to be angry. In situations like I went through, there is always a real danger of allowing anger, resentment, and bitterness to rob us of what God wants to do in and through us during our time of trouble. I do not believe that the Lord did all these things to me, nor do I believe that anyone specifically was "out to get me." I took myself out of God's will and as a result received due recompense for my foolishness. Today I hold no anger toward anyone who accused me. I believe that everyone acted with the best of intentions according to the light that they possessed at the time. Further, I am convinced that the Lord used all of these people and situations to get my attention so that I could be restored to a right relationship with Him and get back to the business of faithfully carrying out His call on my life.

My Restoration Called for Willing Submission to Godly Elders

THE FIRESTORM OF CONTROVERSY that engulfed my ministry beginning in June 1992 was fueled by my own mistakes and the misunderstandings of others. The initial spark was the publication in a Christian magazine of a lengthy cover story that investigated virtually every aspect of my ministry. Particular attention was given to challenging the veracity of my life before I became a Christian as told in my book *The Satan Seller*, published in 1972.

As the fallout from this exposé grew, and acting on the advice of friends and counselors, I invited a group of Christian brothers to convene as a council to examine the charges and accusations against me and to help me design a plan for the future of my ministry. Initially, the council consisted of five men: three pastors, an attorney, and an educator.

At the time I did not have a long-term relationship with any of these brothers; two of them I did not even meet personally until the council convened for the first time in January 1993. One pastor was the man who had performed the wedding ceremony for Susan and me. Because he knew us better than any of the others, he became the de facto leader of the group. I knew one of the other pastors slightly because I had preached at his church on one occasion. The third pastor came on board even though he had never met me, simply because his pastor's heart wanted to help a Christian brother in trouble. With extensive experience as a mediator, the attorney had a wonderful ministry of reconciliation. The educator, who was also an ordained minister, had many years of experience teaching in such areas as teacher training, praise and worship, using motivational gifts, and marriage and family relationships.

From the outset, Susan and I submitted ourselves fully and without reservation to this spiritual oversight and advisory council. We gave them complete authority and freedom to speak into our lives in any area out of their wisdom and spiritual anointing. We believed in the biblical principle of submission to the authority of elders for correction and restoration in love as found in the 18th chapter of Matthew:

> *If your brother sins against you, go and show him his fault, just between the two of you. If he listens to you, you have won your brother over. But if he will not listen, take one or two others along, so that 'every matter may be established by the testimony of two or three witnesses.' If he refuses to listen to them, tell it to the church; and if he refuses to listen even to the church, treat him as you would a pagan or a tax collector* (Matthew 18:15-17).

At first, I was scared to death at the idea of placing myself under authority; I thought it meant that someone would be telling me what to do all the time. I quickly discovered, however, that that's not what submission to authority is all about. If you know the love of Jesus and believe that the Holy Spirit dwells in the heart of every Christian, then you can trust God to put the proper people in place to give you a covering, and to give you guidance. Once you learn that you can actually hear the Lord's voice through these people, then being under authority becomes a liberating situation that doesn't take away from you at all.

I submitted myself in writing, totally, to my advisory council, and said to them, "If you tell me to step down and never speak the name of Jesus again publicly, I'll do that, because I believe in this process, I believe in the Word of God, and I believe in the Holy Spirit's ability to guide me through your counsel." My written statement of submission specifically testifies, in part:

> I accept the authority of the elders to collect charges against me, hear the case and determine the issues. I accept their authority to conduct inquiries into the accusations and dispose of the charges against me according to the principles of the church. I accept

their authority to administer discipline commensu-
rate with the offense or to vindicate and absolve me
in connection with said charges. I recognize the
authority of the elders to impose discipline upon
me that may include repentance, confession, restitution, suspension, cancellation of credentials,
expulsion from the ministry or the church, or both,
public or private reprimand, or such other discipline
as may be appropriate including suspension or
deferment of discipline during a period of proba-
tion. I place no restriction on the disciplinary authority of the elders.[1]

One of the first things they told me was to be quiet and
not try to defend myself. They said, "If anyone has questions,
they are to talk to us, not you. We don't want you to have to
spend the rest of your life and ministry talking about this
instead of talking about Jesus." There was great wisdom in
their words, and I followed their counsel.

My Restoration Required Specific Steps of Correction

BEFORE THE COUNCIL MET in January
1993, several months were spent compiling information about
my personal history and public ministry. During their deliber-
ations they determined that the original article attacking me
was "less than fair in representing the truth and that some edi-
torial bias slanted the reporting of the facts 'behind the story.'
" Nevertheless, the council identified numerous problems
within my ministry and organization which required immediate attention.[1]

After the board released their recommendations, I asked
the leaders involved with Warnke Ministries to voluntarily
come under the scrutiny and discipline of the Spiritual Advisory Council. When they declined to do so, I was left with no

choice but to sever all ties and connections, legal or otherwise, with that ministry. My desire to walk in integrity and to salvage my reputation and Christian witness required nothing less. Not long after, Susan and I formed Celebration of Hope, the ministry under which we have operated ever since. In our new ministry, all the recommendations of my Advisory Board have been implemented.

The Long Road Back Is Still a Road Back

ON JANUARY 25, 1993, I ISSUED a public written statement in which I stood by my original testimony as to former satanic involvement. At the same time, I clarified and acknowledged some exaggerations and embellishments in my story that were due to old and perhaps faulty memories as well as deliberate attempts to "protect the innocent." Exaggeration is also an integral part of comedy, but in some cases in my concerts I had stepped over the line, forgetting my responsibilities as a minister of the gospel for the sake of being good at my "job."

In the second part of my statement I publicly confessed to "the previous ungodliness of my personal life, to my multiple divorces and unwise decisions." This was the really tough part. Until I married Susan in 1991, I had never been able to let God really have control of that part of my life. As a result, I went through three marriages and three divorces. I failed as a husband, as a father, and as a friend. Three marriages ended and I was largely to blame. Here is where I really had to eat humble pie. I could not make any excuses or blame anyone except myself. All I could do was confess, repent, and ask for forgiveness.

Even in this, God's grace was sufficient. My past is my past; I can neither deny it nor hide it. I can never undo what was done, but in God's mercy and forgiveness I have been able to "press on toward the goal to win the prize for which God has called me heavenward in Christ Jesus" (Phil. 3:14).

God still has plans for me. All the sins and mistakes of my past combined cannot cancel the gifts or calling of God on my life. In the nine years since we began our long road to recovery, God has blessed our ministry. When we first began Celebration of Hope, we operated on a very small budget. There was not even enough money to set salary schedules. By the grace of God we have grown quietly and steadily until today we are speaking and ministering to more people each year than we did the year before. We are also seeing thousands of people respond to the gospel, many for the first time. For example, in 1997 and 1998, we ministered in 290 services, covering 16 states and five foreign nations, to a total of 57,539 people. Of that number, 14,199 responded to the altar calls, with 579 indicating a first-time conversion to Christ.

At different times along the way, several people have approached me offering to help me return to the "big time." I have declined every such offer, because the "big time" is not where the Lord wants me. The focus of my current ministry is on local churches and fellowships. I may never return to the "big time," and that's fine with me, because I am right now walking in my restoration.

My Advisory Board of spiritual overseers is still in place, and will be for the foreseeable future. Over the years it has expanded from four to seven members, two of whom have been on board from the very beginning. This is an indication of what we've learned about authority. I have been restored, but rather than thinking, "Okay, I've gotten through this; I don't need to be under authority anymore," I want more authority rather than less, because it has been so liberating and empowering. God brought me through the worst time in my life, and He did it through godly men who care about Susan and me and our ministry and who have the right and authority to speak into our lives. That is a spiritual covering that we have no desire to part with.

Our ministry has two boards, a corporate board and a spiritual oversight board, which is the larger of the two. Corporate board members are chosen from the spiritual oversight board. We all meet together once a year. We are in prayer and contact frequently throughout the rest of the time. All the overseers have a Christ-centered focus. There are no "bean counters" on the boards anymore. My accountant is my accountant and has nothing to do with the decision-making process for the ministry. That's just the way it should be. Elders and spiritual overseers make the decisions, while the "functionaries" function. This helps ensure that our ministry stays on track with God's will and purpose.

I'm not saying any of this to brag, unless it's to brag on God. He is good all the time, and He is faithful. The point I'm trying to make is that if God can restore me to useful and effective ministry, He can restore anyone. All it requires is the willingness to humble yourself before God, obey what He says, and listen to the counsel of godly people He brings into your life. The road back may be long, slow, and bumpy, but it *is* a road back. No one can keep you from walking it except you.

God Is Always "Refilling the Willing"

THE WOUNDS INFLICTED by "friendly fire" are not fatal wounds. They hurt terribly and may even cripple you for awhile, but healing comes in time, if you allow it. That's the key. Ultimately, no one stands in the way of your restoration except you. No matter what has happened, no matter how much you have been hurt, no matter how badly you have messed up, you *can* recover. You *can* survive the Church.

God has already made it clear how He feels about you. He loves you and wants to have intimate fellowship with you. His gifts and calling on your life are irreversible; He will never rescind them. If you have been broken by your circumstances, let the healing balm of Christ rebuild you so that you are stronger than you were before. Don't let the world define you. Remember that God's opinion is the only one that matters, and "if God is for us, who can be against us?" (Rom. 8:31b)

Don't allow doubt, fear, or guilt to hold you back. The Lord stands with His arms open, ready to embrace you, to receive you, and to restore you, if you will only come to Him. "Let us then approach the throne of grace with confidence, so that we may receive mercy and find grace to help us in our time of need" (Heb. 4:16).

> Who am I, Lord,
> To once again enter Your house
> Begging forgiveness, expecting understanding?
> Who am I, Lord,
> To once again kneel at Your altar
> Asking for mercy, anticipating Your grace?
> Who am I, Lord,
> To come into Your presence
> And even assume You will forgive;
> To dare believe You will understand?
> Who am I, Lord?
> I am Yours.

As long as you are alive and breathing, you're never too far gone to come back. I'm living proof of that. The Lord is always ready to refill the willing and to restore the humble of heart. Wherever you are right now, and regardless of how far you may have fallen or how battered you are by the "friendly fire" of the *ekklesia*, God still has a plan for your life and He still wants to use you in fulfilling His purpose. The only person who can prevent your restoration is you. Don't miss out on all that God still has in store for you. Submit to Him, trust Him, and obey Him. Let Him raise you up and bring you back into the fullness of His plan and purpose for you. He can reestablish all the power and promise of your original calling, and take you to places that you may have believed were closed to you forever.

There is an ancient Celtic prayer that reads:

King of mysteries, Who was and is, before the elements, before the ages, King Eternal, comely in aspect, Who reigns forever, grant me three things:

Keenness to discern Your will,
Wisdom to understand it,
Courage to follow where it leads.

ENDNOTE

1. The full text of my statement, as well as all documents of the Tribunal Hearing Board, including their findings and recommendations and annual written updates, are posted on my ministry website, www.mikewarnke.org. On the home-page, click on "FAQs."

Additional copies of this book and other
book titles from DESTINY IMAGE are
available at your local bookstore.

For a complete list of our titles,
visit us at www.destinyimage.com
Send a request for a catalog to:

Destiny Image₍ₐ₎ Publishers, Inc.
P.O. Box 310
Shippensburg, PA 17257-0310

*"Speaking to the Purposes of God for This
Generation and for the Generations to Come"*

6B-2:175